Indiana Student Companion

Authors

Robert Q. Berry, III
Associate Professor of Mathematics Education, Department of Curriculum, Instruction and Special Education, University of Virginia, Charlottesville, Virginia

Zachary Champagne
Assistant in Research
Florida Center for Research in Science, Technology, Engineering, and Mathematics (FCR-STEM)
Jacksonville, Florida

Eric Milou
Professor of Mathematics
Rowan University, Glassboro, New Jersey

Jane F. Schielack
Professor Emerita
Department of Mathematics
Texas A&M University
College Station, Texas

Jonathan A. Wray
Mathematics Instructional Facilitator, Howard County Public Schools, Ellicott City, Maryland

Randall I. Charles
Professor Emeritus
Department of Mathematics
San Jose State University
San Jose, California

Francis (Skip) Fennell
L. Stanley Bowlsbey Professor of Education and Graduate and Professional Studies, McDaniel College
Westminster, Maryland

PEARSON

Glenview, Illinois Boston, Massachusetts Chandler, Arizona New York, New York

PEARSON

ISBN-13: 978-0-328-91692-4
ISBN-10: 0-328-91692-7
7 20

CONTENTS

ACKNOWLEDGEMENTS

Photographs

Photo locators denoted as follows: Top (T), Center (C), Bottom (B), Left (L), Right (R), Background (Bkgd)

001 (TC) Antonioguillem/Fotolia; (TL) lucadp/Fotolia; **002** Michaeljung/Fotolia; **005** littlestocker/Fotolia; **007** (CL) Windu/Fotolia; (CR) Dmytro Sandratskyi/Fotolia; (TR) BillionPhotos/Fotolia; (TL) Olga Kovalenko/Fotolia; (TC) Indigolotos/Fotolia; **008** (TC) Konstantin Sutyagin/Fotolia; (TR) Lisa F. Young/Fotolia; **009** Sam Spiro/Fotolia; **011** (TCR) Jenifoto/Fotolia; (TR) Kimberly Reinick/Fotolia; (TCL) Sarawutk/Fotolia; (CL) trinetuzun/Fotolia; (BCL) Gitusik/Fotolia; (BL) Lvonne Wierink/Fotolia; **012** roger ashford/Fotolia; **014** Sam Spiro/Fotolia; **015** Sascha Burkard/Fotolia; **018** Jipen/Fotolia; **020** Fotomek/Fotolia; **033** (TC) Axpitel/Fotolia; (CL) Soulart/Shutterstock; (C) Miro Novak/Shutterstock; **037** John Lund/Blend Images/Getty Images; (BCL) nortongo/Fotolia; **038** Lesya Dolyuk/Shutterstock.

Explore It!

ACTIVITY

Charlene has 2 flash drives of the same size that she uses to store pictures and videos. Each drive is holding the same number of gigabytes (GB) of data, *d*. Charlene wants to move everything to a memory card that can hold up to 8 GB.

Indiana Lesson 1
Solve Inequalities

Go Online | PearsonRealize.com

I can...
solve inequalities that require multiple steps.

A. Charlene is going to delete 1 GB of data from each flash drive. How can the total amount of data left on the two flash drives be represented as an expression?

B. How can the expression you wrote be used to write an inequality that shows the maximum amount of data each flash drive can have on it in order to have all of the data transfer to the 8-GB memory card?

Focus on math practices

Reasoning If each flash drive has 5 GB of memory, can all of the data be transferred to the memory card? Explain.

? Essential Question How is solving a multi-step inequality similar to and different from solving a multi-step equation?

EXAMPLE 1 Write and Solve Multi-Step Inequalities

Scan for Multimedia

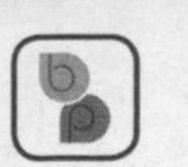

Gabriela likes to make people guess her age. She gives them this clue:

Add 13 to the product of 3 and the sum of my age and 2 you get a number greater than my height in inches.

What are possible ages for Gabriela? Graph the solution.

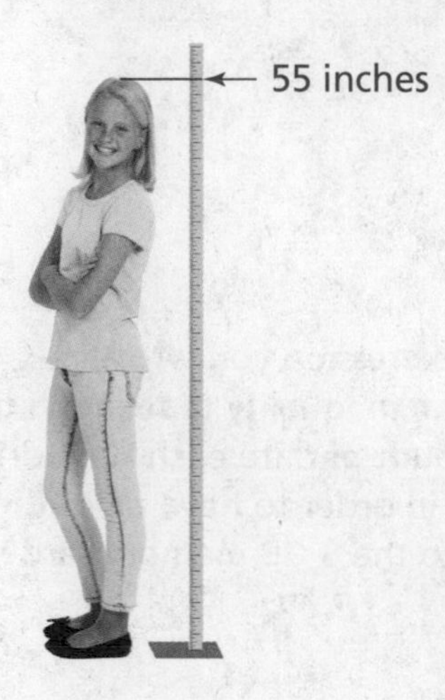

STEP 1 Write an inequality to represent Gabriela's age, x.

Multiply by 3		The sum of Gabriela's age and 2		Add 13	>	Gabriela's height
3	·	$(x + 2)$	+	13	>	55

STEP 2 Solve the inequality. Then graph the solution.

$3(x + 2) + 13 > 55$

$3x + 6 + 13 > 55$ — Use the Distributive Property.

$3x + 19 > 55$

$3x + 19 - 19 > 55 - 19$

$\frac{3x}{3} > \frac{36}{3}$ — Use the Subtraction and Division Properties of Inequality to isolate the variable.

$x > 12$

Gabriela is more than 12 years old.

Try It!

Twice the difference of Felipe's age, f, and 4 is at least 2. What are possible values for Felipe's age? Graph the solution.

Write the inequality. ☐ (☐) ○ ☐

Use the Distributive Property to rewrite the inequality as $2f -$ ☐ ≥ 2.

Solve the inequality.

$2f \geq$ ☐

$f \geq$ ☐

Graph the solution.

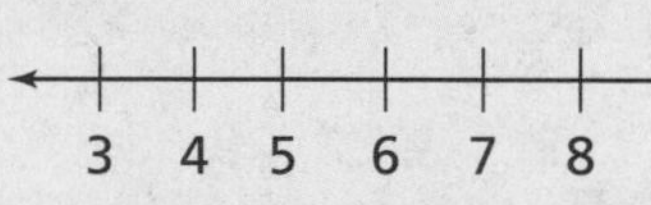

Convince Me! Describe the similarity between the process of solving an inequality with two steps and solving an inequality with more than two steps.

EXAMPLE 2  Solve More Multi-Step Inequalities

  ACTIVITY  ASSESS

Solve the inequality $-3(x + 4) + 3 \geq 9$. Then graph the solution.

$-3(x+4)+3 \geq 9$

$-3x - 12 + 3 \geq 9$

$-3x - 9 \geq 9$

$-3x \geq 18$

$\frac{-3x}{-3} \leq \frac{18}{-3}$

$x \leq -6$

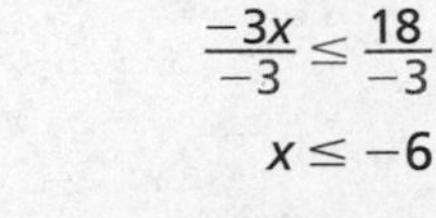

Remember to use the Distributive Property.

Remember: When multiplying or dividing by a negative value, the inequality symbol is reversed.

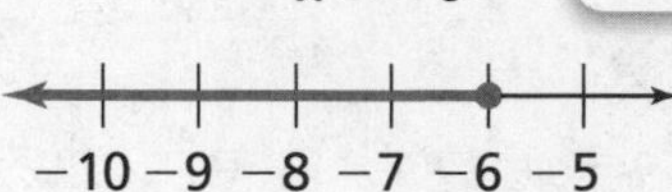

EXAMPLE 3  Solve Multi-Step Inequalities by Combining Like Terms

Solve the inequality $2(3.5t - 2) + 6t \geq -2$. Then graph the solution.

$2(3.5t-2)+6t \geq -2$

$7t - 4 + 6t \geq -2$

$13t - 4 \geq -2$

$13t - 4 + 4 \geq -2 + 4$

$13t \geq 2$

$t \geq \frac{2}{13}$

Distribute and then combine like terms.

Use the Division Property of Inequality.

0 $\quad \frac{2}{13} \quad$ 1

Try It!

Solve the inequality $-1 - 6(6 + 2x) < 11$. Then graph the solution.

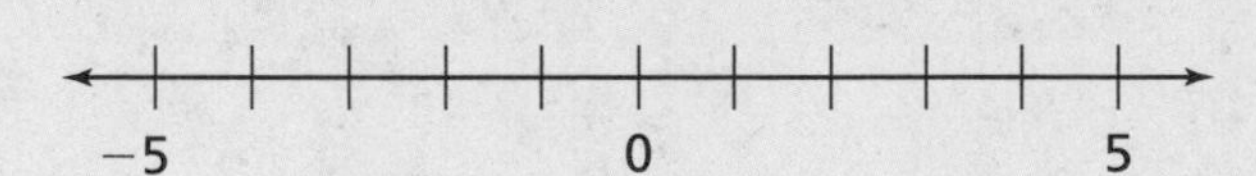

Solve the inequality $3(4 - 6) + 2 \geq 2(-t + 3) + 4$. Then graph the solution.

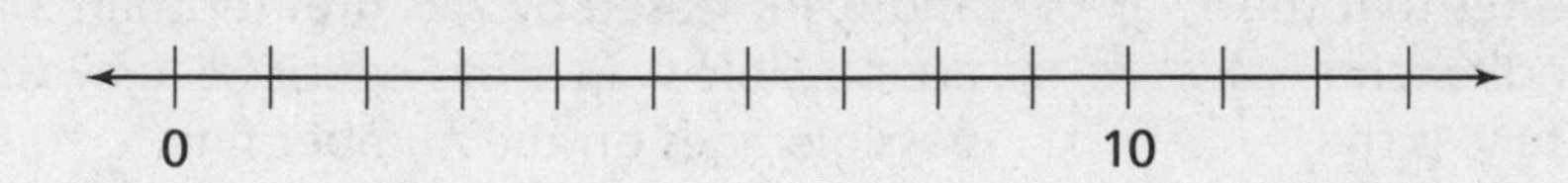

KEY CONCEPT

Solving multi-step inequalities is similar to solving multi-step equations. You may need to use the Distributive Property, combine like terms, and/or use inverse relationships and properties to solve them.

$4(y-4)+8 \leq 20$

$4y-16+8 \leq 20$

$4y-8 \leq 20$

$4y-8+8 \leq 20+8$

$4y \leq 28$

$\frac{4y}{4} \leq \frac{28}{4}$

$y \leq 7$

Do You Understand?

1. **Essential Question** How is solving a multi-step inequality similar to and different from solving a multi-step equation?

2. **Be Precise** Explain how you would combine like terms and use properties of operations to solve the inequality $5(2t+3)-3t<16$.

3. **Critique Reasoning** Gloria's solution to a multi-step inequality is $r>7$. She states that the graph will have an open dot at 7 and extend with an arrow to the right indefinitely. Is she correct? Explain.

Do You Know How?

4. Solve the inequality $2(n+3)-4<6$. Then graph the solution.

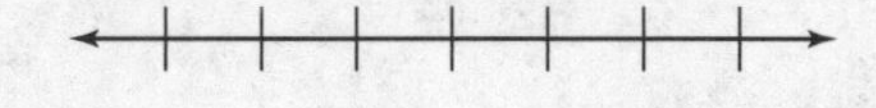

5. Solve the inequality $-2(x+3)+2 \geq 6$. Then graph the solution.

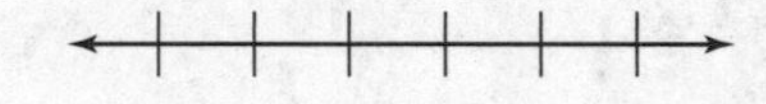

6. Three times the difference of Federico's age and 4, increased by 7, is greater than 37. What are possible values of Federico's age? Graph his possible ages on the number line.

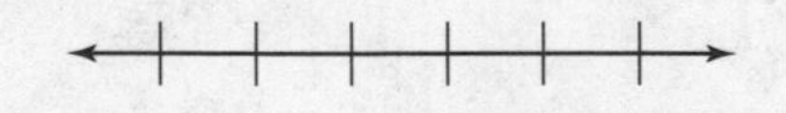

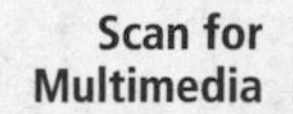
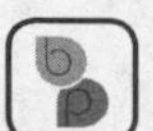

Name: ________________________________

Practice & Problem Solving

Scan for Multimedia

7. Use the inequality $18 < -3(4x - 2)$.

a. Solve the inequality for x.

b. Which graph shows the solution to the inequality?

Ⓐ 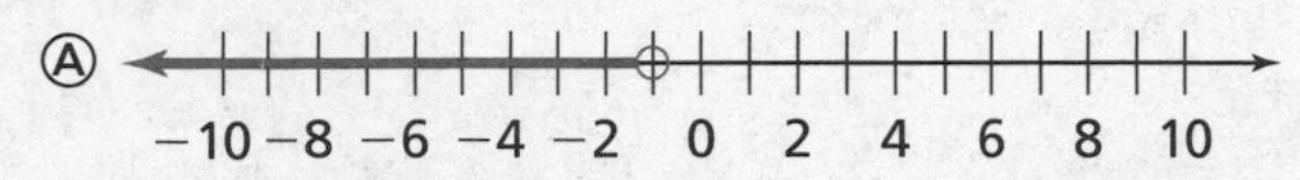

Ⓑ −10 −8 −6 −4 −2 0 2 4 6 8 10

Ⓒ −10 −8 −6 −4 −2 0 2 4 6 8 10

Ⓓ −10 −8 −6 −4 −2 0 2 4 6 8 10

8. Michelle says that the solution to the inequality $2(4y - 3) > -22$ is $y > -3.5$. Her work is shown.

$$2(4y - 3) > -22$$
$$8y > -28$$
$$y > -3.5$$

a. What was Michelle's mistake?

b. What is the solution to the inequality?

9. Model with Math The length of a picture frame is 7 inches more than the width. For what values of x is the perimeter of the picture frame greater than 154 inches?

10. Critique Reasoning Sierra says that she can simplify the left side of the inequality $2(-3 + 5) + 2 \geq -4(x - 2) - 3$ by combining the terms within the parentheses, but that she cannot do the same on the right side. Is Sierra correct? Explain.

11. a. Solve the inequality $30 \geq 6\left(\frac{2}{3}z + \frac{1}{3}\right)$.

b. Solve the inequality $15.6 < 2.7(z - 1) - 0.6$.

c. Are there any values of z that are solutions to both inequalities? Use a number line to support your answer.

12. Mr. Lin baked banana bread for a bake sale to raise money for the math team. He said that he added a spoonful of walnuts for each of the students in his three classes, and that he added more than 250 walnuts. He used the inequality $16w + 24w + 10w > 250$ to represent the situation, where w represents the number of walnuts in each spoonful. How many walnuts could be in each spoonful?

13. Use both the Addition and Multiplication Properties of Inequality to solve the inequality. Graph the solution on a number line.

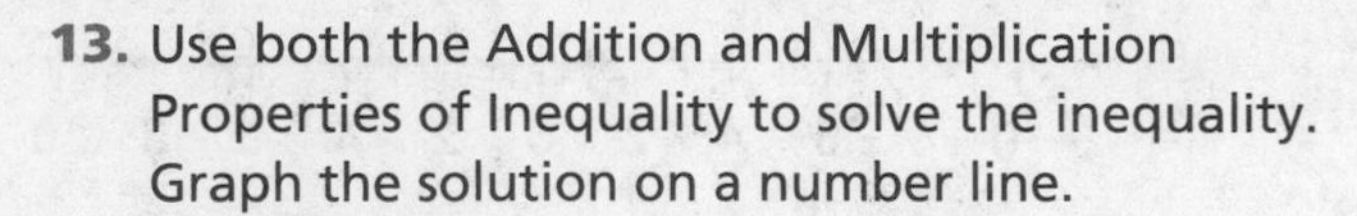

$2(3y - 5) < -16$

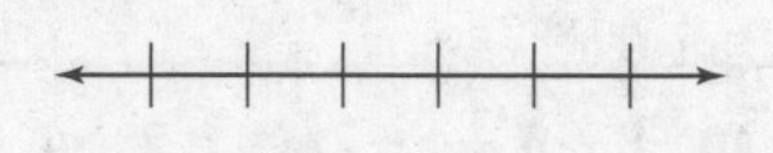

14. **Higher Order Thinking** Solve each of the given inequalities for z. Which of the inequalities has 5 as a solution?

Inequality 1	Inequality 2
$4(2.8z + 1.75) > -26.6$	$2(1.9z + 1.5) \leq 18.2$

Assessment Practice

15. Solve the inequality. Explain how you found your answer.

$$4(x - 2) - 3 \geq -3(-2 + 6) + 2$$

Indiana Lesson 2

Outcomes of Compound Events

Go Online | PearsonRealize.com

I can...
find all possible outcomes of a compound event.

Solve & Discuss It!

ACTIVITY

Cameron packed two pairs of shorts and three T-shirts for a weekend trip. What are some combinations of shirts and shorts that Cameron can wear while on his trip? How many days will he have a different outfit to wear?

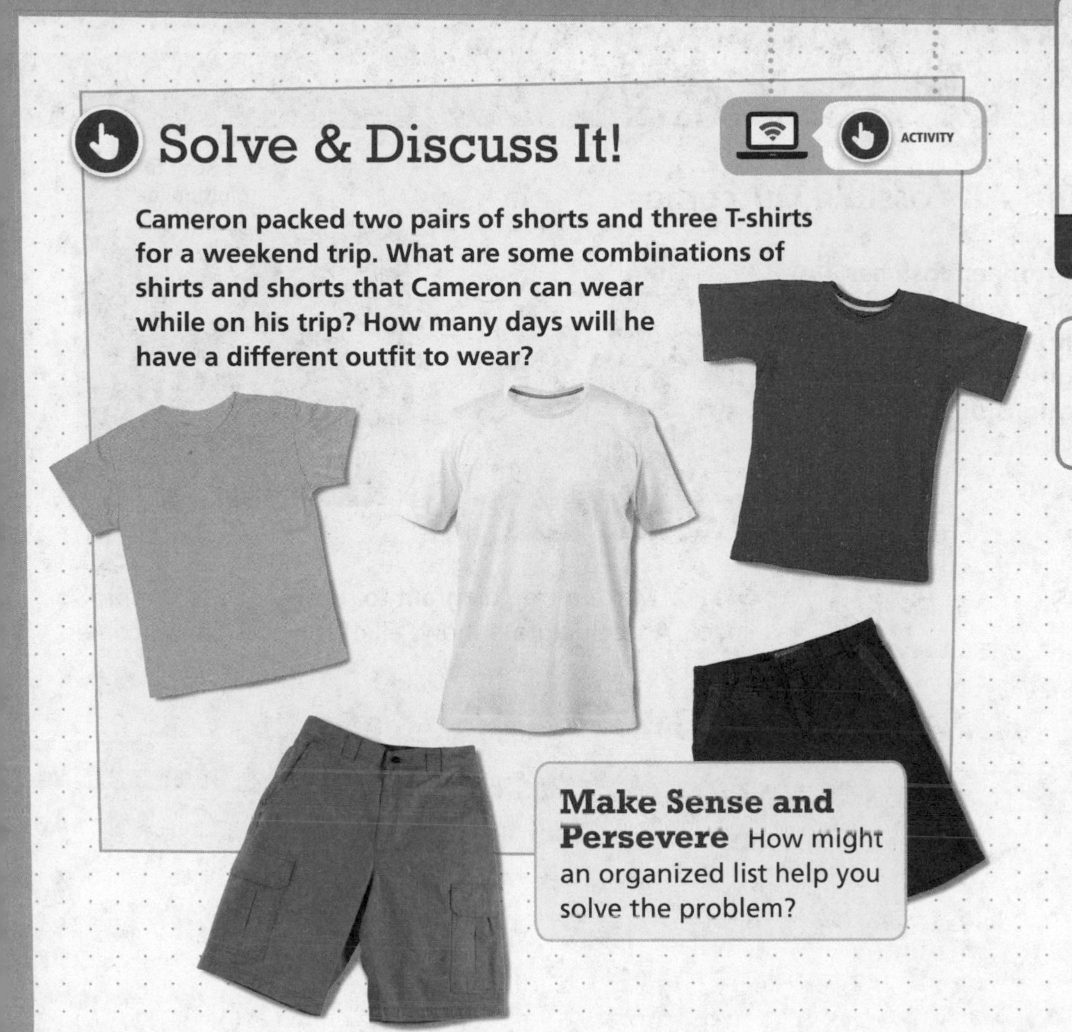

Make Sense and Persevere How might an organized list help you solve the problem?

Focus on math practices

Reasoning How would the number of different outfits change if Cameron packed a pair of khaki shorts? Explain.

Essential Question How can all of the possible outcomes, or the sample space, of a compound event be represented?

EXAMPLE 1

Find All Possible Outcomes

Hailey has two sisters and no brothers. Josh has two brothers and no sisters. They wonder what the chances are, in a family with three children, that the children will be all boys or all girls. How can they determine all possible combinations of boys and girls in a family with three children?

STEP 1 List the different events.

Child 1 is either a boy or a girl.

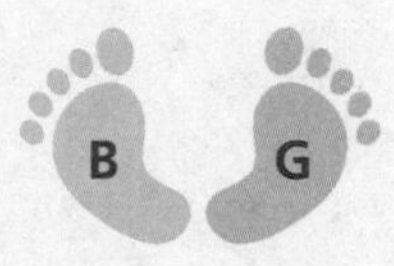

Child 2 is either a boy or a girl.

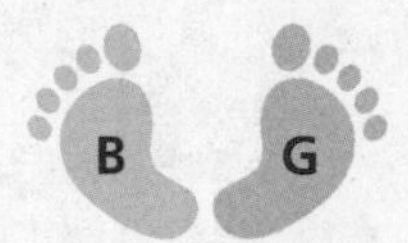

Child 3 is either a boy or a girl.

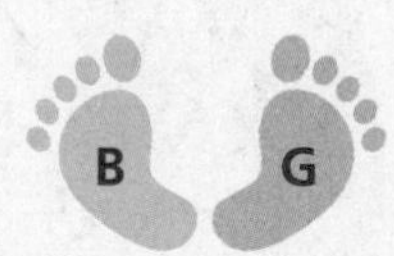

This is a *compound event*. A **compound event** consists of two or more events. This compound event consists of three events.

STEP 2 Make a tree diagram to represent the sample space. A tree diagram shows all of the possible outcomes.

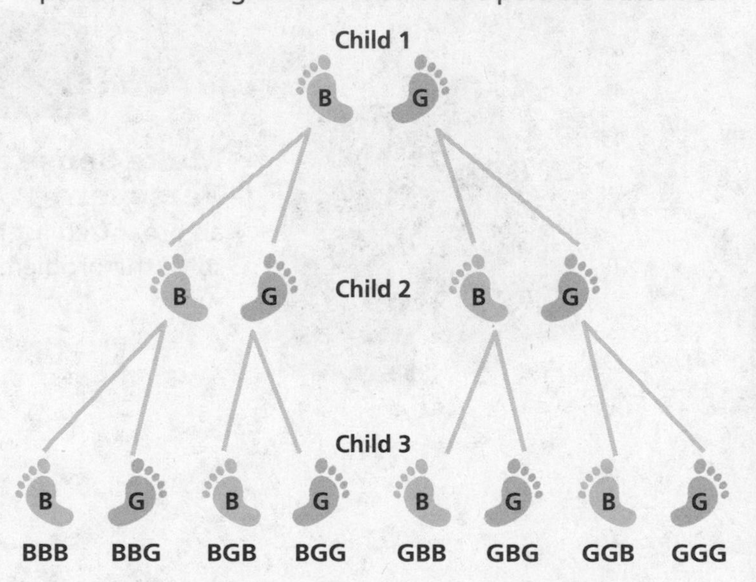

Hailey and Josh can make a tree diagram to show the sample space of boys and girls in a family with three children.

Try It!

Jorge will flip two quarters at the same time. Complete the tree diagram, and then list the sample space of this compound event. Use H for heads and T for tails.

The sample space is:

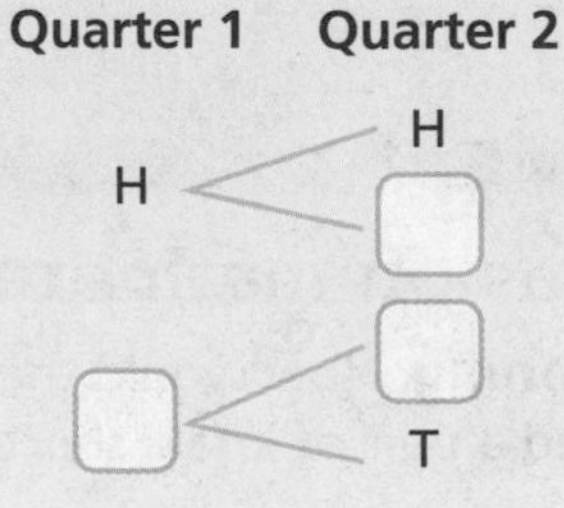

Convince Me! How does the sample space change when the number of quarters that Jorge flips is increased by 1?

EXAMPLE 2  Use a Table to Represent Sample Spaces

ACTIVITY ASSESS

A game is played by spinning the two spinners shown. Players match the results of the spinners to combinations on their game cards. How many different combinations are possible?

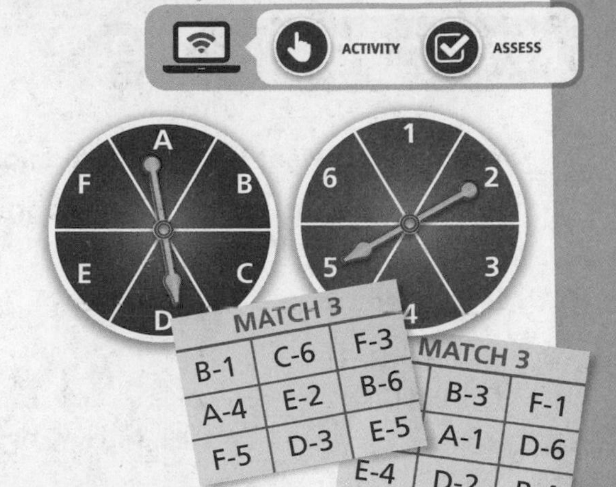

Use a table to represent the sample space.

Remember: The sample space shows all of the possible outcomes.

	1	2	3	4	5	6
A	A-1	A-2	A-3	A-4	A-5	A-6
B	B-1	B-2	B-3	B-4	B-5	B-6
C	C-1	C-2	C-3	C-4	C-5	C-6
D	D-1	D-2	D-3	D-4	D-5	D-6
E	E-1	E-2	E-3	E-4	E-5	E-6
F	F-1	F-2	F-3	F-4	F-5	F-6

The **Multiplication Counting Principle** says that if there are *m* outcomes for one event and *n* outcomes for another, then their combined outcomes can be found by multiplying *m* times *n*.

There are 6 letters and 6 numbers.

$6 \times 6 = 36$ outcomes

There are 36 different letter–number combinations.

The sample space consists of 36 possible outcomes.

EXAMPLE 3  Use an Organized List to Represent Sample Spaces

Stan will roll a number cube labeled 1 to 6 and flip a coin.

How many outcomes are there? What are all of the possible outcomes?

Use the Multiplication Counting Principle to find the total number of outcomes.

There are 6 possible outcomes for the number cube.

There are 2 possible outcomes for the coin.

$6 \times 2 = 12$

There are 12 possible outcomes.

Use an organized list to represent all of the possible outcomes, or the sample space.

{(1, H), (1, T),
(2, H), (2, T),
(3, H), (3, T),
(4, H), (4, T),
(5, H), (5, T),
(6, H), (6, T)}

Try It!

The bag contains tiles labeled with the letters A, B, and C. The box contains tiles labeled with the numbers 1, 2, and 3. June draws one letter tile and one number tile. Use the Multiplication Counting Principle to find the number of possible outcomes and then represent the sample space using either a table or an organized list.

KEY CONCEPT

A compound event is a combination of two or more events.

An organized list, table, or tree diagram can be used to represent the sample space of a compound event.

Organized List

{(H, H), (H, T), (T, H), (T, T)}

Table

	H	T
H	H, H	H, T
T	T, H	T, T

Tree Diagram

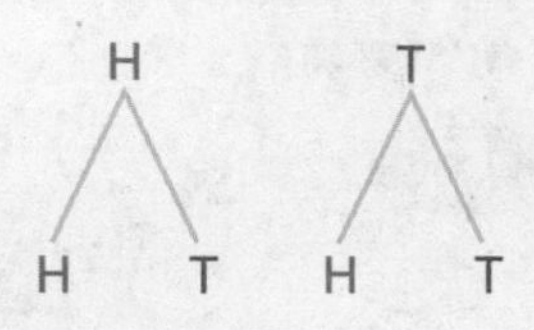

The Multiplication Counting Principle can be used to find the total number of possible outcomes for a compound event.

There are 2 possible outcomes for flipping a coin.

$2 \times 2 = 4$

There are 4 possible outcomes for flipping two coins.

Do You Understand?

1. **Essential Question** How can all of the possible outcomes, or the sample space, of a compound event be represented?

2. **Generalize** Will a list, a table, and a tree diagram always give you the same number of outcomes for the same compound event? Explain.

3. **Use Structure** How can a table help you understand why the Multiplication Counting Principle can be used to find the total number of possible outcomes?

Do You Know How?

4. Both spinner A and spinner B have equal-size sections, as shown at the right.

Spinner A

Spinner B

   a. Use the Multiplication Counting Principle to find the total number of possible outcomes when both spinners are spun.

   b. Make a table to represent the sample space when both spinners are spun.

5. Tiles labeled with the letters X, Y, and Z are in a bag. Tiles labeled with the numbers 1 and 2 are in a box.

   Make a tree diagram to represent the sample space of the compound event of selecting one tile from each container.

Name: ____________________

Practice & Problem Solving  

Scan for Multimedia

Leveled Practice In 6 and 7, find the number of possible outcomes for each event.

6. Oliver is playing a game in which he has to choose one of two numbers (2 or 7) and then one of five vowels (a, e, i, o, or u). How many possible outcomes are there?

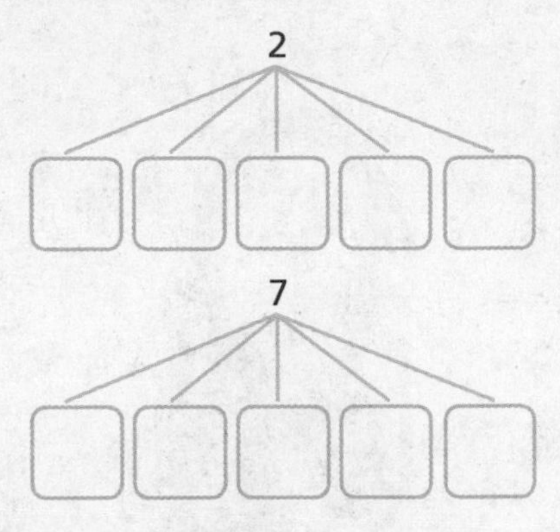

There are ☐ possible outcomes.

7. There are four stores that sell school supplies (S1, S2, S3, and S4) and three stores that sell sporting goods (G1, G2, and G3) nearby. How many possible combinations of stores could you visit to buy a tennis racquet and then a backpack?

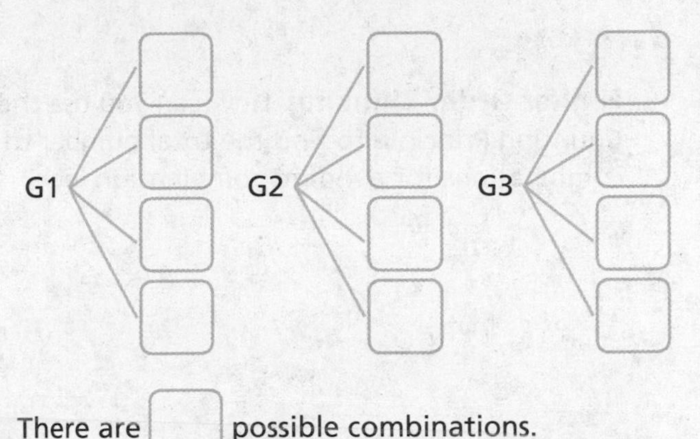

There are ☐ possible combinations.

8. A bakery sells wheat, multigrain, rye, and oat bread. Each type of bread is available as a loaf or as dinner rolls.

a. Complete the table to show all of the possible outcomes for the types and styles of bread sold by the bakery.

b. Find the number of possible outcomes.

	Loaf	Rolls
Wheat		
Multi-grain		
Rye		
Oat		

9. Generalize How does the number of possible outcomes of a single event help you determine the total number of possible outcomes of a compound event?

10. A new car can be purchased with a choice of four exterior colors (A, B, C, and D) and three interior colors (1, 2, and 3). Use the Multiplication Counting Principle to find the total number of possible color combinations for the car. Then show the sample space.

11. Two friends each plan to order a fruit drink at the diner. The available flavors are kiwi (K), lemon (L), and watermelon (W). Make a list to represent all of the possible outcomes of the friends' fruit drink order. Write each outcome in the format (Friend 1, Friend 2).

12. An 8th-grade class has 12 female students and 14 male students. One female and one male will be randomly chosen to represent the class in a math competition. How many combinations of one female and one male can be made from the students in the 8th-grade class? Explain.

13. Higher Order Thinking How can you use the Multiplication Counting Principle to find the total number of possible combinations for a 4-digit combination lock?

Assessment Practice

14. Complete the table to show the sample space of two-digit numbers using the digits 8, 4, 3, and 2.

	8	4	3	2
8				
4				
3				
2				

How many possible outcomes are there?

15. Complete the table to show the sample space of number–letter combinations using the numbers 7, 8, and 9, and the letters R, S, T, U, V, and W.

	R	S	T	U	V	W
7						
8						
9						

How many possible outcomes are there?

Solve & Discuss It!

Talia is playing a game in which she must choose Option 1 or Option 2 and then spin the game wheel, flip the coin, and roll the number cube labeled 1 through 6. For her to win a prize, all of the conditions listed under the chosen option must occur. Which option should Talia choose? Explain.

Option 1	Option 2
• The game wheel lands on S.	• The game wheel lands on Z.
• The coin lands on tails.	• The coin lands on either side.
• An even number is rolled.	• The number 3 is rolled.

Look for Relationships
How can you use what you know about sample spaces to choose the best option?

Indiana Lesson 3
Find Probabilities of Independent Events

Go Online | **PearsonRealize.com**

I can...
find probability of independent events.

Focus on math practices

Make Sense and Persevere Suppose an Option 3 was added to the game, with the conditions that the game wheel lands on Q, the coin lands on either side, and an odd number is rolled. Should Talia change her choice to Option 3? Explain.

? **Essential Question** How can a model help in finding the probability of two independent events?

EXAMPLE 1  Find the Probability of Independent Events

Scan for Multimedia 

Sadie has one ticket left at the school fair and she has not yet won a prize. What is the probability of Sadie winning a prize with *Flip 'n' Spin*?

These two events are independent events. The outcome of a coin toss is independent of the outcome of spinning the spinner.

Use Structure Does having more possible outcomes make it more likely or less likely to win?

ONE WAY Use a table to determine the probability of winning a prize playing *Flip 'n' Spin*.

	Heads (H)	Tails (T)
Red (R)	R, H	R, T
Yellow (Y)	Y, H	Y, T
Blue (B)	B, H	B, T
Green (G)	G, H	G, T

There are 8 possible outcomes.

There is 1 favorable outcome: heads, blue.

$P(\text{heads, blue}) = \frac{1}{8}$ or 12.5%

ANOTHER WAY Determine the probability of each event to find the probability of the two independent events.

When tossing the coin, there are 2 possible outcomes and 1 favorable outcome.

$$P(\text{heads}) = \frac{1}{2}$$

When spinning the spinner, there are 4 possible outcomes and 1 favorable outcome.

$$P(\text{blue}) = \frac{1}{4}$$

You can multiply the two probabilities to find the probability of winning the game.

$$P(\text{heads, blue}) = \frac{1}{2} \times \frac{1}{4} = \frac{1}{8} \text{ or } 12.5\%$$

The probability of Sadie winning a prize is 1 in 8, or 12.5%.

Try It!

The designer of *Flip 'n' Spin* creates a new game using a 5-section spinner, as shown. How does the new spinner change the probability of winning a prize?

Using the 5-section spinner, the probability of winning a prize is ______ × ______ = ______, or ______.

It is ______ likely that a player will win a prize when using the 5-section spinner than when using the 4-section spinner.

Convince Me! What generalization can you make about the number of sections on the spinner and the probability of winning a prize while playing the *Flip 'n' Spin* game?

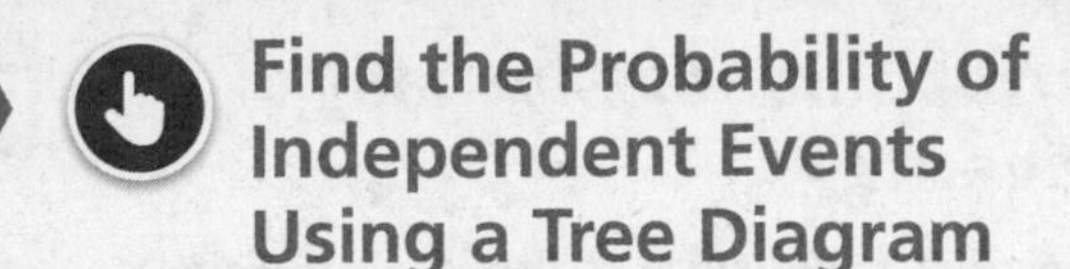

EXAMPLE 2 Find the Probability of Independent Events Using a Tree Diagram

What is the probability that a coin flipped three times will land tails up all three times?

Flip 1

Flip 2

Flip 3

Outcomes	HHH	HHT	HTH	HTT	THH	THT	TTH	TTT

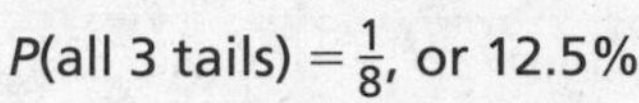

P(all 3 tails) $= \frac{1}{8}$, or 12.5%

The probability of the coin landing tails up is $\frac{1}{2}$.

The probability of the coin landing tails up two times in a row is $\frac{1}{2} \times \frac{1}{2}$ or $\frac{1}{4}$.

The probability of the coin landing tails up three times in a row is $\frac{1}{2} \times \frac{1}{2} \times \frac{1}{2}$ or $\frac{1}{8}$.

Try It!

Is it more likely that a coin flipped three times will land heads up exactly once or will land heads up exactly twice? Explain using probability.

EXAMPLE 3 Find the Complement of an Event

What is the probability that a coin tossed three times will NOT land tails up all three times?

One of the 8 outcomes is 3 tails up.

P(all 3 tails) $= \frac{1}{8}$

Seven of the 8 outcomes are not 3 tails up.

This is the complement of the event, that is, all of the outcomes that are not the desired outcome.

The probability that a coin tossed three times will NOT land tails up all three times is *P*(not 3 tails) $= 1 - \frac{1}{8} = \frac{7}{8}$.

Try It!

Kacie will toss two coins. What is the probability of the two coins landing heads up? What is the probability of the two coins NOT landing heads up?

EXAMPLE 4 Find the Probability of Mutually Exclusive Events

Shannon will roll two number cubes numbered 1 to 6. What is the probability that the sum of the numbers rolled is either even or equal to 11?

STEP 1 Use a table to list the possible outcomes.

	1	2	3	4	5	6
1	2	3	4	5	6	7
2	3	4	5	6	7	8
3	4	5	6	7	8	9
4	5	6	7	8	9	10
5	6	7	8	9	10	11
6	7	8	9	10	11	12

Even sums are shaded red.

Sums equal to 11 are shaded yellow.

Eighteen outcomes have even sums.

$P(\text{even sum}) = \frac{18}{36} = \frac{9}{18}$

Two outcomes have a sum of 11.

$P(\text{sum} = 11) = \frac{2}{36} = \frac{1}{18}$

11 is an odd number, so a sum of 11 cannot be even. These two events are **mutually exclusive.**

STEP 2 Add the two probabilities.

$P(\text{even sum OR sum} = 11) = \frac{9}{18} + \frac{1}{18} = \frac{10}{18}$ or $\frac{5}{9}$

EXAMPLE 5  Find the Probability of Events that Are Not Mutually Exclusive

Quincy will roll two number cubes numbered 1 to 6. What is the probability that the sum of the numbers rolled is either even or greater than 10?

STEP 1 Use a table to list the possible outcomes.

	1	2	3	4	5	6
1	2	3	4	5	6	7
2	3	4	5	6	7	8
3	4	5	6	7	8	9
4	5	6	7	8	9	10
5	6	7	8	9	10	11
6	7	8	9	10	11	12

One outcome is even and greater than 10. These events are not mutually exclusive.

Eighteen outcomes have even sums.

$P(\text{even sum}) = \frac{18}{36}$

Three outcomes have sums greater than 10.

$P(\text{sum greater than } 10) = \frac{3}{36}$

STEP 2 Add the probabilities of even sums and sums greater than 10, and then subtract the probability of any outcomes that are **both** even sums **and** sums greater than 10.

Even sums | Sums > 10 | Even sum greater than 10

$\frac{18}{36} + \frac{3}{36} - \frac{1}{36} = \frac{20}{36}$

Try It!

Jamie will roll two number cubes numbered 1 to 6 and find the sums. Are these events mutually exclusive?

a. rolling sums of 6 and multiples of 3?

b. rolling odd sums and multiples of 2?

KEY CONCEPT

Two events are independent if the outcome of one event does NOT affect the outcome of the other event.

To determine the probability of two independent events, multiply the probabilities of each event.

Do You Understand?

1. **Essential Question** How can a model help in finding the probability of two independent events?

2. **Generalize** How can you use the probability of the desired outcome to find the complement of an event?

3. How does finding the probability of rolling two number cubes and getting a 6 on each number cube compare to finding the probability of rolling a 6 on either number cube?

Do You Know How?

4. One of three contestants will be randomly selected to win a prize. One of three different prizes will be randomly awarded to the contestant whose name is selected to win. The tree diagram shows all possible outcomes of this contest.

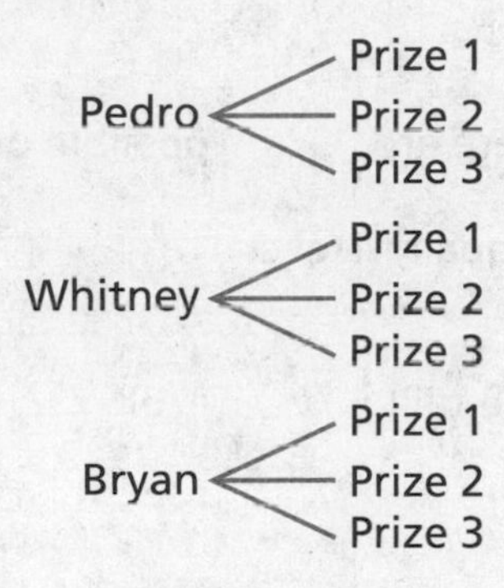

What is the probability that Whitney will win prize 2?

5. The table shows all of the possible outcomes for flipping a coin and spinning the pointer of a spinner with four equal-size sections labeled 1 through 4.

	1	2	3	4
Heads	heads, 1	heads, 2	heads, 3	heads, 4
Tails	tails, 1	tails, 2	tails, 3	tails, 4

a. What is the probability that the pointer will NOT stop on 3 and the coin will NOT land on heads?

b. What is the probability that either the coin will land on heads or the spinner will land on 3?

Name: ____________________

Practice & Problem Solving

Scan for Multimedia

Leveled Practice **In 6 and 7, find the probability of each event.**

6. A fair coin is tossed twice in succession. The sample space is shown, where H represents heads up and T represents tails up. Find the probability of getting exactly one tail.

(Toss 1, Toss 2)	
(H, H)	(T, H)
(H, T)	(T, T)

There are ☐ outcomes that have exactly one tail. There are ☐ possible outcomes, which are equally likely.

P(exactly one tail) = ☐, or ☐ %

7. The tree diagram shows the sample space of two-digit numbers that can be created using the digits 2, 6, 7, and 9. What is the probability of choosing a number from the sample space that contains both 9 and 6?

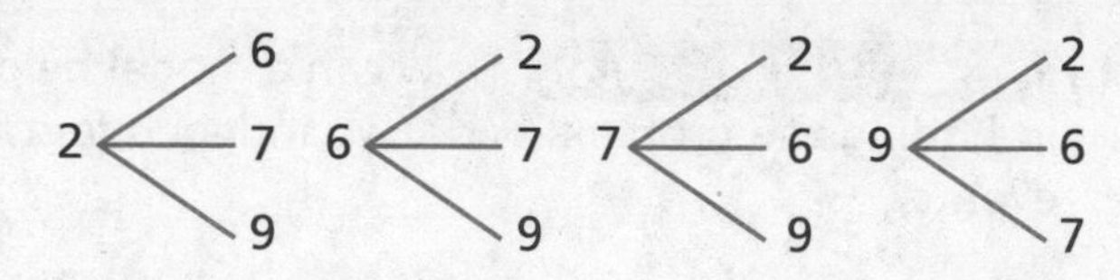

There are ☐ outcomes that include both 9 and 6. There are ☐ possible outcomes, which are equally likely.

P(9 and 6) = ☐, or ☐ %

8. The table shows the possible outcomes of spinning the given spinner and flipping a fair coin. Find the probability of the coin landing heads up and the pointer landing on either 1, 2, or 4.

	1	2	3	4	5
H	H, 1	H, 2	H, 3	H, 4	H, 5
T	T, 1	T, 2	T, 3	T, 4	T, 5

9. The organized list shows all of the possible outcomes when three fair coins are flipped. The possible outcomes of each flip are heads (H) and tails (T).

a. What is the probability that at least 2 fair coins land heads up when 3 are flipped?

b. What is the probability that at least 2 fair coins do NOT land heads up when 3 are flipped?

Sample Space
HHH
HHT
HTH
HTT
THH
THT
TTH
TTT

10. Hashi has a set of cards numbered 1–8. He puts the numbers 1–4 in one bag and the numbers 5– 8 in another. He then pulls a card from each bag to make a two-digit number, using a number from the first bag for the first digit and a number from the second bag for the second digit.

a. Complete the table to show the possible outcomes.

b. What is the probability that the two-digit number will be even or a multiple of 5?

c. What is the probability that the two-digit number will be a multiple of 4 or a multiple of 9?

		First Digit			
		1	2	3	4
Second Digit	5				
	6				
	7				
	8				

11. Critique Reasoning Thomas puts 2 red marbles, 4 blue marbles, and 3 yellow marbles in a bag. He will pull a marble out of the bag three times, each time putting the marble back in the bag before pulling out a new one. He says that it would be impossible to pull a red marble all three times because there are only 2 red marbles in the bag. Is Thomas's reasoning correct? If not, what is the probability of pulling a red marble all three times. Explain.

12. When tossing a coin two times, is the probability of the coin landing heads up both times the same as the probability of the coin NOT landing tails up both times? Explain.

13. A teacher brings a bag of 15 apples and 5 oranges on a field trip. A student randomly pulls one piece of fruit from the bag, replaces it, and then pulls another piece of fruit from the bag.

a. What is the probability that both pieces of fruit will be apples?

b. What is the probability that the student will NOT pull two apples from the bag?

c. What is the probability that the student will pull two pieces of fruit, neither of which are apples?

14. Look for Relationships Gary spins two game wheels at the carnival. He will win a prize if both of the wheels land on any red section. How does the chance of winning change if different game wheels are used with fewer red sections?

15. Model with Math Elena won a shirt from a local clothing store. The store will randomly choose a sleeve type (long, short, no sleeve) and a color (gray, blue, pink) for the prize. Elena doesn't like long sleeve shirts or the colors pink and blue. Draw a tree diagram to represent the sample space. Then find the probability that the free shirt will NOT have long sleeves and will be neither pink NOR blue?

16. Higher Order Thinking The table shows the sample space of picking a two-character password using the letters Y, B, R, O, G, and P. If double letters are not allowed, what is the probability of choosing a password with no Y's? With no O's? Is one probability greater than the other? Explain.

Possible Combinations					
Y, B	B, R	R, O	O, G	G, P	P, Y
Y, R	B, O	R, G	O, P	G, Y	P, B
Y, O	B, G	R, P	O, Y	G, B	P, R
Y, G	B, P	R, Y	O, B	G, R	P, O
Y, P	B, Y	R, B	O, R	G, O	P, G

Assessment Practice

17. A single number cube is rolled twice and the two numbers are added.

PART A

Find the probability of rolling two numbers that have a sum equal to 10.

PART B

What is the probability of rolling two numbers that have a sum that is either even or less than 5?

First Roll \ Second Roll	1	2	3	4	5	6
1	2	3	4	5	6	7
2	3	4	5	6	7	8
3	4	5	6	7	8	9
4	5	6	7	8	9	10
5	6	7	8	9	10	11
6	7	8	9	10	11	12

Indiana Lesson 4
Find Probabilities of Dependent Events

Go Online | PearsonRealize.com

I can...
find the probability of dependent events.

Solve & Discuss It!

Sasha and Diego are setting up the duck pond game at the school fair. On Friday, every time a student pulls a winning duck from the pond, Sasha and Diego will put it back in the pond before the next student plays the game. On Saturday, every time a student pulls a winning duck from the pond, they decide to leave it out. On which night would you have a better chance of winning a prize?

Construct Arguments Why does the probability of winning change if the winning duck is not replaced?

Focus on math practices

Use Structure If there are 50 ducks in the pond and 10 are winning ducks, what is the probability that the first player will win? If the winning duck is not returned to the pond, what is the probability that both the first player and the second player will win?

? **Essential Question** How can you find the probability of dependent events?

EXAMPLE 1  Understand Dependent Events

A bag contains the marbles shown. Dakota chooses one marble from the bag without looking. Without replacing the first marble, she chooses a second marble from the bag. What is the probability that she chooses a red marble and then a purple marble?

Use Structure How does the probability change when the marble is not replaced?

ONE WAY Define the sample space by listing all of the possible outcomes. Then find the probability.

First Marble	Second Marble

There are 6 possible outcomes. One outcome is red then purple.

$P(\text{red then purple}) = \frac{1}{6}$

ANOTHER WAY Multiply the probabilities of each event.

$P(\text{red}) = \frac{1}{3}$

$P(\text{purple after red}) = \frac{1}{2}$

The red marble is not replaced, so there are 2 marbles left, 1 of which is purple.

$P(\text{red then purple}) = P(\text{red}) \cdot P(\text{purple after red})$

$= \frac{1}{3} \cdot \frac{1}{2} = \frac{1}{6}$

Because the first marble chosen is not replaced, the possible outcomes for the second choice are affected. These events are **dependent events** because the occurrence of the first event affects the probability of the second event.

Try It!

All three marbles are returned to the bag. What is the probability that Dakota will choose a purple marble and then a red marble?

$P(\text{purple}) = \frac{\square}{\square}$ $P(\text{red after purple}) = \frac{\square}{\square}$ $P(\text{red then purple}) = \frac{\square}{\square} \cdot \frac{\square}{\square} = \frac{\square}{\square}$

Convince Me! Why does the number of possible outcomes change after each selection?

ACTIVITY

ASSESS

EXAMPLE 2  Find the Probability of Dependent Events

Phil and Marie are among six students who are eligible for the drawing for one of two tickets to a baseball game. One name will be drawn at random from the six names. Then a second name will be drawn at random from the remaining names. What is the probability that both Marie's name and Phil's name will be drawn?

STEP 1 Find the probability of one of their names being drawn for the first ticket.

$P(\text{Marie or Phil}) = \frac{2}{6} = \frac{1}{3}$

There are two favorable outcomes out of six possible outcomes.

STEP 2 Assuming either Marie's name or Phil's name is drawn on the first round, find the probability of the other person's name being drawn for the second ticket.

$P(\text{Phil given Marie or Marie given Phil}) = \frac{1}{5}$

There is one favorable outcome out of five possible outcomes.

STEP 3 Multiply the two probabilities to find the probability of both Marie **and** Phil winning the two tickets.

$P(\text{Marie and Phil}) = \frac{1}{3} \times \frac{1}{5} = \frac{1}{15}$

The probability of both Marie and Phil winning the two tickets is $\frac{1}{15}$ or about 7%.

Generalize How is the second event dependent on the outcome of the first event?

EXAMPLE 3  Find the Probability of Multiple Events

The tiles shown are placed in a bag. Angie will draw one tile at a time from the bag without looking and without replacing the tile drawn.

C M A M A H
T A T E I

What is the probability that the first three tiles she draws are the three "A" tiles?

On the first draw, there are 3 tiles with the letter A out of a total of 11 tiles.

$P(A) = \frac{3}{11}$

M A T H E M A T I C A

Assuming the first draw is an "A" tile, on the second draw, there are 2 "A" tiles out of a total of 10 tiles.

$P(A) = \frac{2}{10}$

M A T H E M A T I C

Assuming the first and second draws are "A" tiles, on the third draw, there is 1 "A" tile out of a total of 9 tiles.

$P(A) = \frac{1}{9}$

M A T H E M T I C

The probability of drawing the three "A" tiles in a row is

$P(\text{A and A and A}) = \frac{3}{11} \times \frac{2}{10} \times \frac{1}{9} = \frac{6}{990} = \frac{1}{165}$.

What is the probability that Angie draws the two "T" tiles on the first two draws?

KEY CONCEPT

Two events are dependent if the outcome of the first event affects the outcome of the second event.

To determine the probability of dependent events, multiply the probabilities of each event.

Do You Understand?

1. **Essential Question** How can you find the probability of dependent events?

2. **Construct Arguments** Renee says that rolling a number cube twice and getting a 6 both times is an example of dependent events because getting a 6 on the second roll depends on getting a 6 on the first roll. Is Renee correct? Explain.

3. Seven marbles are placed into a bag. What is the probability of randomly pulling a blue marble out of the bag? How does the probability of pulling out a blue marble change if the first marble is not replaced before you pull out a second marble? Explain.

Do You Know How?

In 4–6, use the marbles shown in Exercise 3.

4. What is the probability of pulling two marbles out of the bag and both marbles being green?

5. What is the probability of pulling two marbles out of the bag and both marbles being blue?

6. If the first marble is not replaced after it is pulled out of the bag, what is the probability of pulling out one green marble and then one blue marble?

7. Rashid is shown five envelopes, two of which contain a prize. If he is permitted to choose two envelopes, what is the probability that he will win both prizes?

8. Three friends have entered a contest to win tickets to a concert. If 10 people have entered the contest and 3 winning names are chosen, what is the probability that all three friends will win tickets?

Name: ______________________________

Practice & Problem Solving

Scan for Multimedia

Leveled Practice

9. The letters C, A, and T are placed in a bag. Each letter is randomly drawn from the bag and not replaced. Complete the table to show the sample space. What is the probability that the letters will be drawn out of the bag in the correct order to spell cat?

Probability of pulling C out of the bag first: $\frac{\square}{\square}$

Probability of pulling A out of the bag second: $\frac{\square}{\square}$

Probability of pulling T out of the bag third: $\frac{\square}{\square}$

Probability of C, then A, then T: $\frac{\square}{\square}$

First Draw	Second Draw	Third Draw

10. A red apple, a green apple, and an orange are in a bag. Yasmin randomly pulls one piece of fruit out of the bag and eats it. She then randomly pulls a second piece of fruit out of the bag. Complete the table to show the sample space. What is the probability that both pieces of fruit that Yasmin pulls out of the bag are apples?

Probability of pulling an apple out of the bag first: $\frac{\square}{\square}$

Probability of pulling an apple out of the bag second: $\frac{\square}{\square}$

Probability that both pieces of fruit pulled out of the bag are apples: $\frac{\square}{\square}$

First Piece of Fruit	Second Piece of Fruit

11. A teacher is randomly handing out tests. There are 2 different versions of the test, Test A and Test B. If there are 8 tests in all and an equal number of each version, what is the probability that the first 4 students will all receive Test A?

12. Reasoning There are 2 red marbles and 2 blue marbles in a bag. Kiera pulls a marble out the bag and keeps it. Then her friend Will pulls a marble out of the bag. Is there a better chance that their marbles are the same color or that they are different colors? Explain.

13. A soccer coach has 14 players on her team. Two of the players have experience playing goalie. For an upcoming game, the coach has been asked to randomly choose 2 players to play for the other team to even out the numbers. What is the probability that both of the players chosen will be the players with experience playing goalie?

14. Gwen has a stack of cards with the digits 1–9 on them. She shuffles the cards and places them facedown in a pile.

a. Gwen chooses two cards from the pile to make a two-digit number. She uses the first card as the first digit in the number and the second card as the second digit. What is the probability that Gwen will make the number 15?

b. **Make Sense and Persevere** How would the probability of making 15 change if Gwen could use either card that she chose as the first digit and the other card as the second digit? Explain.

c. Gwen chooses three cards to make a three-digit number. She uses the first card as the first digit in the number, the second card as the second digit, and the third card as the third digit. What is the probability that Gwen will make the number 123?

d. **Reasoning** What is the probability that Gwen randomly chooses two cards from the pile and makes the number 11? Explain.

15. Irene is playing a game. She is shown 3 cups. A ball is hidden under 1 of the 3 cups. Irene has to choose the cup with the hidden ball. If she chooses the wrong cup, that cup is removed and she chooses again. What is the probability that Irene will choose the wrong cup both times?

16. **Higher Order Thinking** A bag contains 6 marbles. Some of the marbles are red and some of the marbles are blue. The probability of pulling out 2 blue marbles without replacement is $\frac{1}{15}$. How many blue marbles and how many red marbles are in the bag?

Assessment Practice

17. Twelve students signed up for the school talent show. Three students plan to sing, four students plan to dance, and the remaining students plan to play an instrument. The director of the show will randomly choose the order of the first two acts. Calculate the probability of each pair of dependent events.

a. *P*(singing then dancing)

b. *P*(singing then *not* dancing)

c. *P*(both playing an instrument)

d. *P*(neither playing an instrument)

e. *P*(both dancing)

Indiana Lesson 5
Attributes of 3-Dimensional Figures

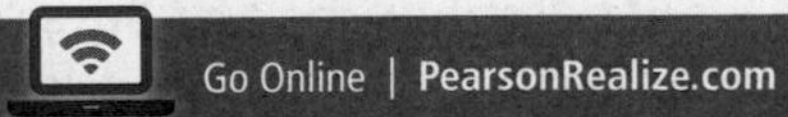

I can...
describe attributes of prisms, cylinders, cones, spheres, and pyramids.

Solve & Discuss It!

ACTIVITY

James is helping his younger sister build a prism with these wooden tools.

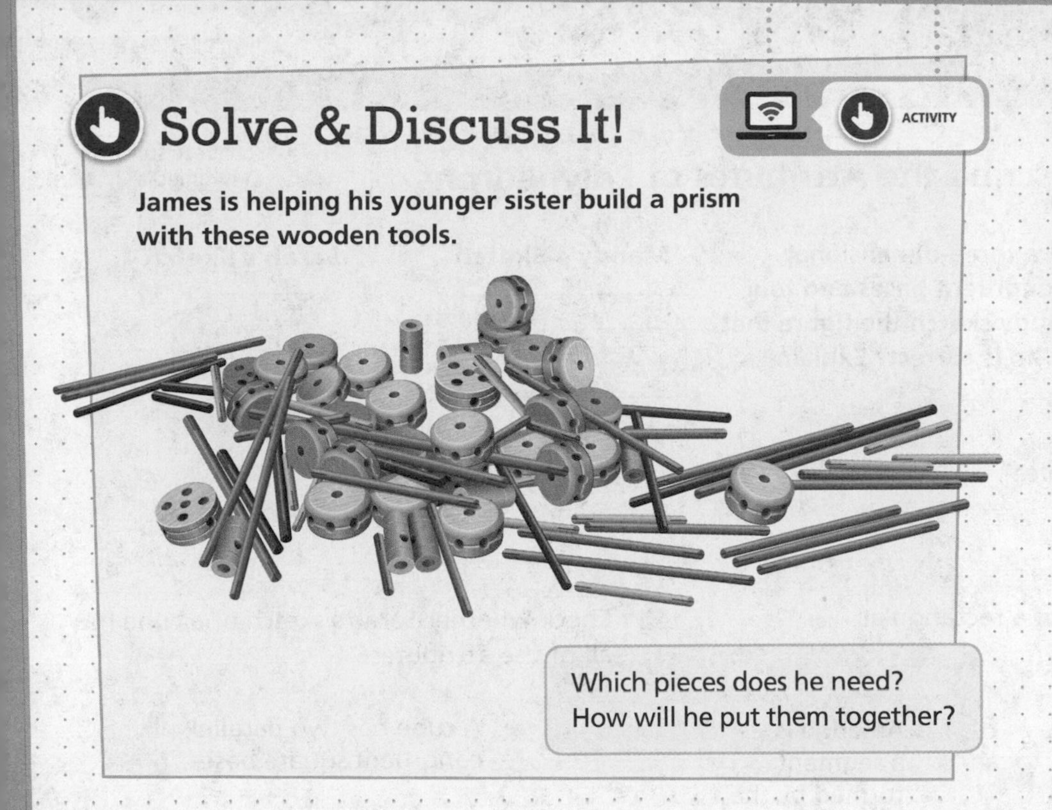

Which pieces does he need?
How will he put them together?

Focus on math practices

Look for Relationships Are all of the prisms that you and your classmates described exactly the same? Explain.

? **Essential Question** What attributes describe three-dimensional figures?

EXAMPLE 1 Describe the Attributes of Polyhedrons

Scan for Multimedia

Jared describes the attributes of a three-dimensional polyhedron with two parallel, congruent bases and four rectangular faces. Sarah and Mandy sketch the figure that they think Jared is describing. Who is correct? Explain.

Mandy's Sketch

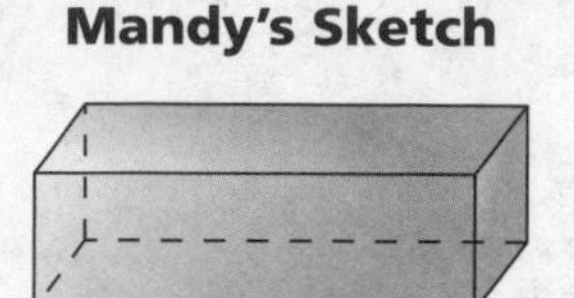

Sarah's Sketch

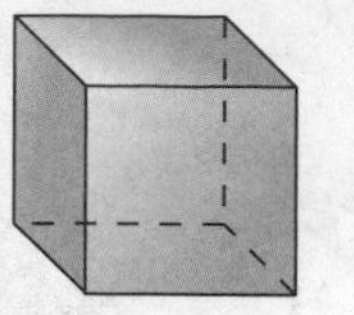

Construct Arguments
How can you explain your choice?

Check whether Mandy's sketch of a rectangular prism has all of the attributes.

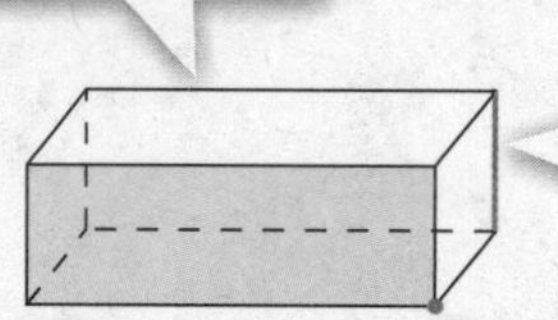

A prism has two parallel, congruent bases. This prism has rectangular bases.

An **edge** is a segment formed by the intersection of two faces. This prism has 12 edges.

A prism has rectangular lateral faces. A lateral face is any face or surface that is not a base. This prism has four rectangular lateral faces.

A **vertex** is a point where three or more edges come together. This prism has 8 vertices.

Check whether Sarah's sketch of a cube has all of the attributes.

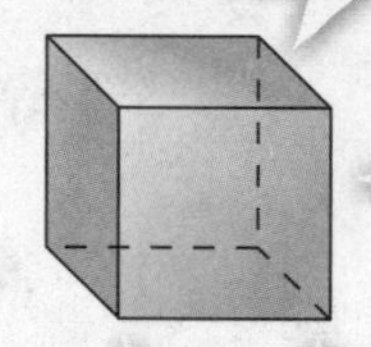

A cube has two parallel, congruent square bases.

A cube has four square lateral faces.

A cube has 8 vertices and 12 edges.

Because a square is also a rectangle, both figures have the attributes Jared described. Mandy and Sarah are both correct.

Try It!

Describe the attributes of the pyramid.

This pyramid has [ ] square base.

This pyramid has [ ] triangular lateral faces.

This pyramid has [ ] edges.

This pyramid has [ ] vertices.

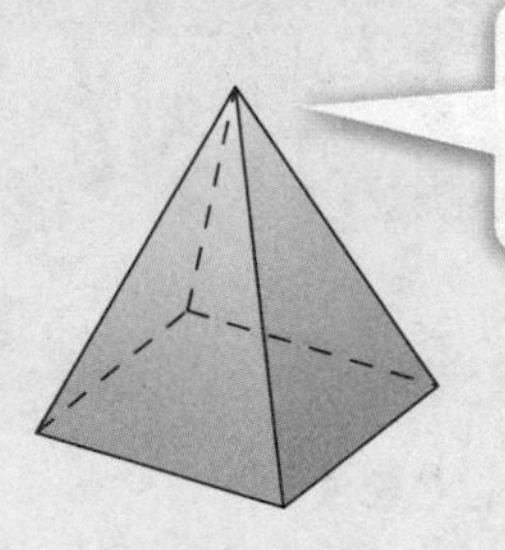

The vertex where all of the triangular faces meet is called the *apex*.

Convince Me! Use attributes to describe how prisms and pyramids are alike and how they are different.

EXAMPLE 2  Describe the Attributes of Cylinders and Cones

Describe the attributes of the cylinder and the cone.

A.

A cylinder has two parallel, congruent circular bases.

A cylinder has a curved surface.

Because the surfaces are all curved, a cylinder has no edges or vertices.

B.

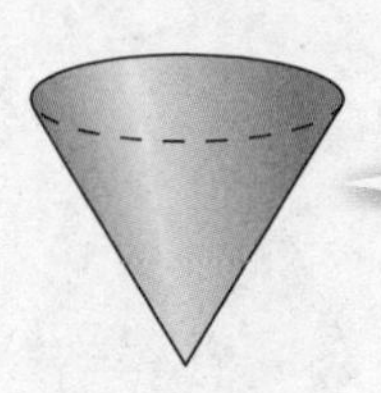

A **cone** is a three-dimensional figure that has one circular base that tapers to a point, often called its vertex.

A cone has one circular base and one vertex. It has no edges.

EXAMPLE 3  Describe the Attributes of Spheres

How can you describe the attributes of a sphere?

A **sphere** is a round three-dimensional figure in which every point on its surface is the same distance from its center.

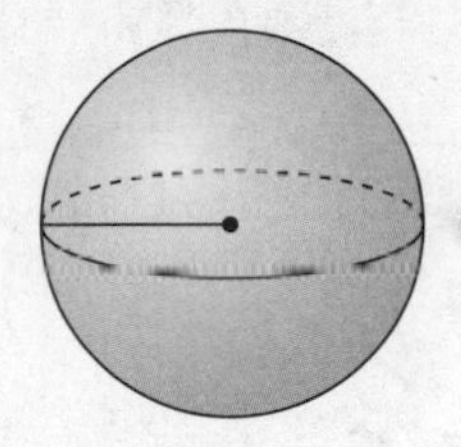

A sphere has a round surface, so it has no bases, faces, edges, or vertices.

Try It!

Complete the table to describe the attributes of each figure.

	cone	cylinder	rectangular pyramid	sphere	hexagonal prism
Number of Bases					
Number of Lateral Faces					
Number of Edges					
Number of Vertices					

KEY CONCEPT 

Three-dimensional figures can be described by bases, lateral faces, edges, and vertices.

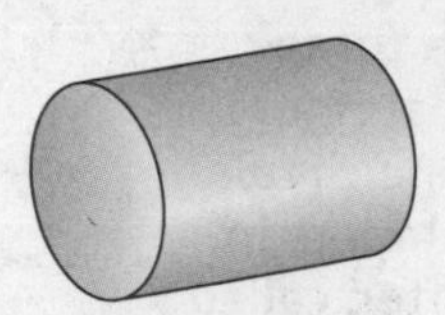

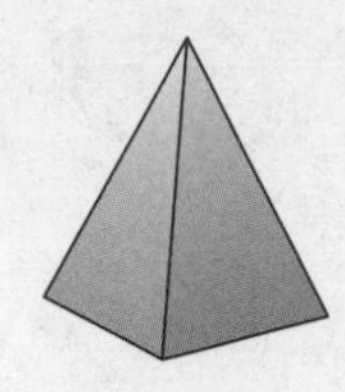

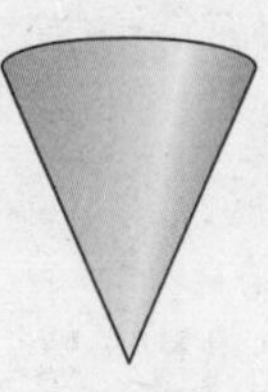

Do You Understand?

1. What attributes describe three-dimensional figures?

2. Use attributes to describe how a cone and a cylinder are different.

3. **Be Precise** Ray is describing a three-dimensional figure that does not have any bases, lateral faces, edges, or vertices. What else does he need to add to his description so that the only possible figure he could be describing is a sphere?

Do You Know How?

4. A three-dimensional figure has two parallel bases and four lateral faces. The parallel bases and lateral faces are all the same size and shape. Name the figure.

5. Describe the attributes of a square pyramid.

In 6–9, identify the number of vertices in each three-dimensional figure.

6. rectangular prism

7. cone

8. sphere

9. triangular pyramid

  PRACTICE  TUTORIAL

Name: ______________________________

Practice & Problem Solving  

Scan for Multimedia 

Leveled Practice **In 10–13, describe the attributes of the figure shown.**

10.

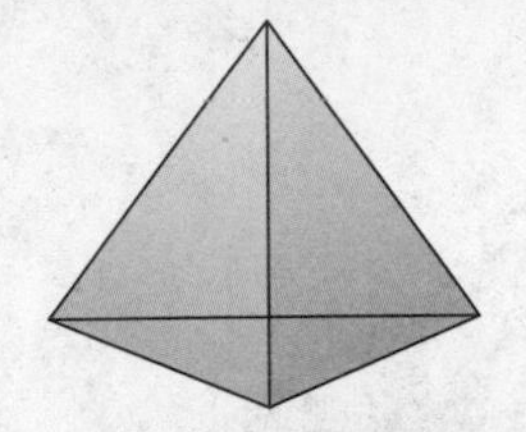

The pyramid has 1 ____ base.

The pyramid has ____ triangular lateral faces.

The pyramid has 4 ____.

The pyramid has ____ edges.

11.

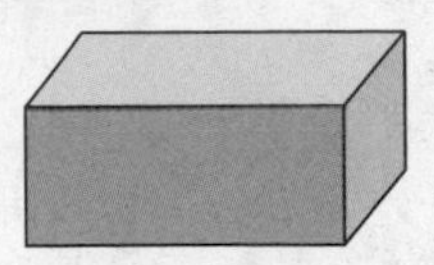

The prism has ____ rectangular bases.

The prism has 4 rectangular lateral ____.

The prism has ____ vertices.

The prism has 12 ____.

12.

13.

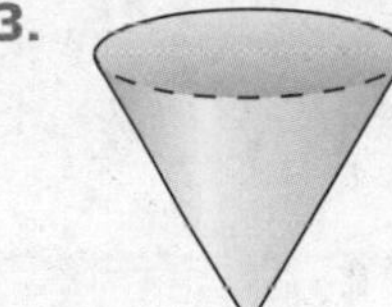

In 14–17, name the three-dimensional figure with the given attributes.

14. 2 triangular parallel bases, 3 rectangular lateral faces

15. 0 bases, 0 lateral faces, 0 edges, 0 sides; Every point on the surface is the same distance from the center.

16. 1 square base, 4 triangular lateral faces

17. 2 parallel square bases, 4 square lateral faces

18. **Construct Arguments** Sasha described a shape with two parallel, congruent triangular bases. Could Sasha's shape be a pyramid? Explain.

19. Which three-dimensional shapes have at least one circular base?

20. Samuel is building with magnetic tiles. He builds a three-dimensional figure using 3 identical square tiles and 2 identical triangular tiles. Name the three-dimensional figure that Samuel created.

21. Elise made a figure out of clay that does not have any edges. Which figures could she have made?

22. Georgia made a cardboard house. She combined two three-dimensional figures to create a house, as shown. Describe the attributes of the two figures that Georgia used.

23. **Higher Order Thinking** Describe the figure shown.

Assessment Practice

24. Complete the table to describe the attributes of each figure.

	sphere	triangular prism	pentagonal prism	cone
Number of Bases				
Number of Lateral Faces				
Number of Edges				
Number of Vertices				

Solve & Discuss It!

How could Mrs. Mendoza divide the ream of paper equally between two art classes? She has a paper cutter to slice the paper, if needed. What will the dimensions for each sheet of paper be once she has divided the ream? How many sheets will each class receive?

Indiana Lesson 6

Cross Sections

Go Online | PearsonRealize.com

I can...
determine what the cross section looks like when a 3-dimensional figure is sliced.

Focus on math practices

Use Structure How would the number of sheets of paper each class receives change if Mrs. Mendoza started with 300 sheets?

? Essential Question How do the faces and surfaces of a three-dimensional figure determine the two-dimensional shapes created by slicing the figure?

EXAMPLE 1 Describe Cross Sections of Right Rectangular Prisms

Scan for Multimedia

Rachel and Francesca went to a restaurant that serves rectangular bread rolls. Each girl sliced her roll in a different way. What do the *cross sections* look like?

Use Structure Which faces are parallel to the slice?

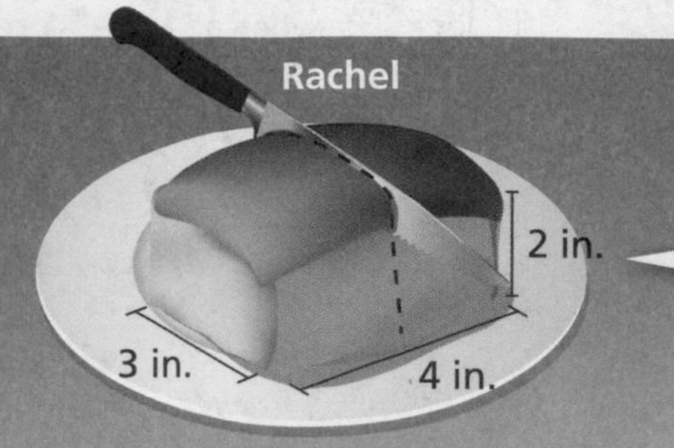

A **cross section** is the two-dimensional shape that is exposed when a slice is made through a three-dimensional object.

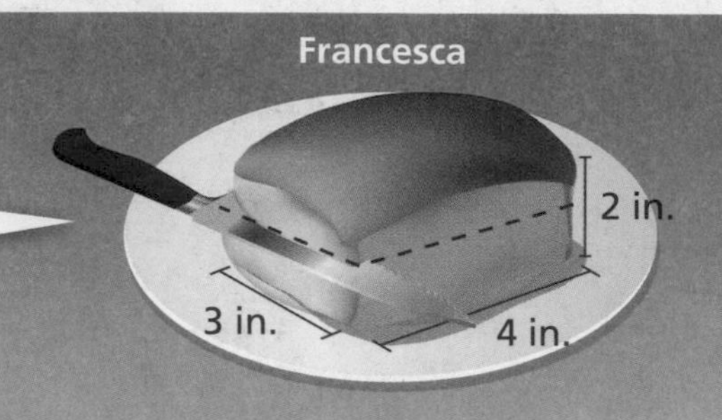

Rachel made a vertical slice that was parallel to the front and back faces of the roll.

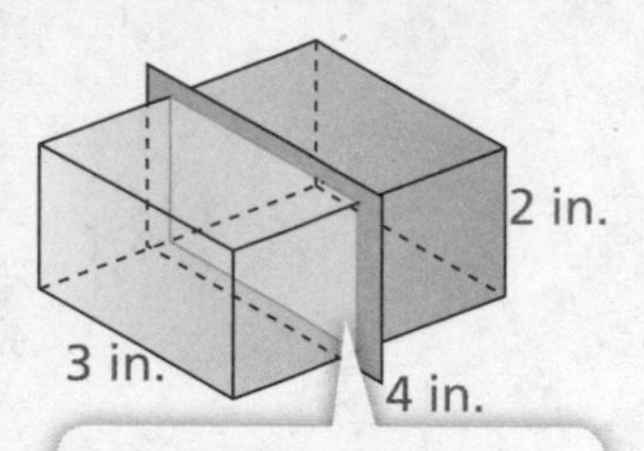

The cross section is parallel to the front and back faces, so it is the same shape as those faces.

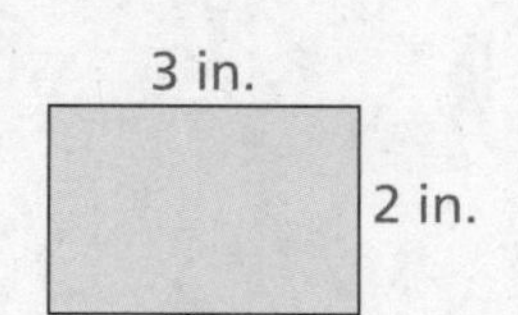

The cross section is a rectangle that is 3 inches by 2 inches.

Francesca made a horizontal slice that was perpendicular to the front and back faces of the roll.

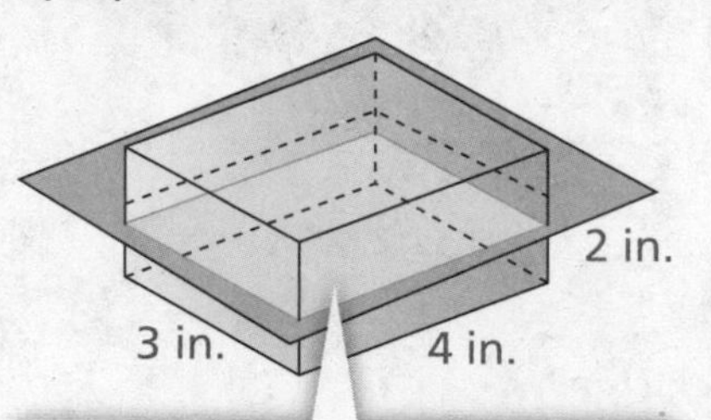

The cross section is parallel to the top and bottom faces, so it is the same shape as those faces.

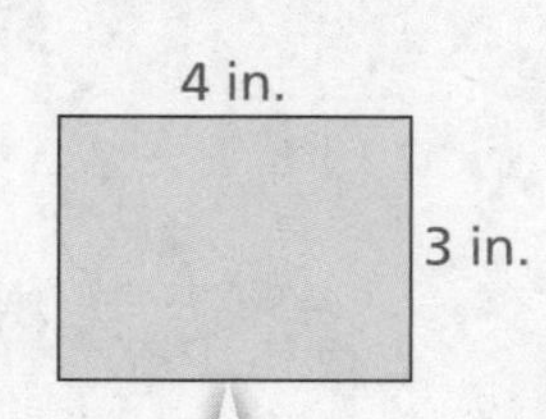

The cross section is a rectangle that is 4 inches by 3 inches.

Try It!

Zachary made a vertical slice that was parallel to the left and right faces of a bread roll. What shape is the cross section, and what are its dimensions?

The shape of the cross section is a ________

that is ________ inches by ________ inches.

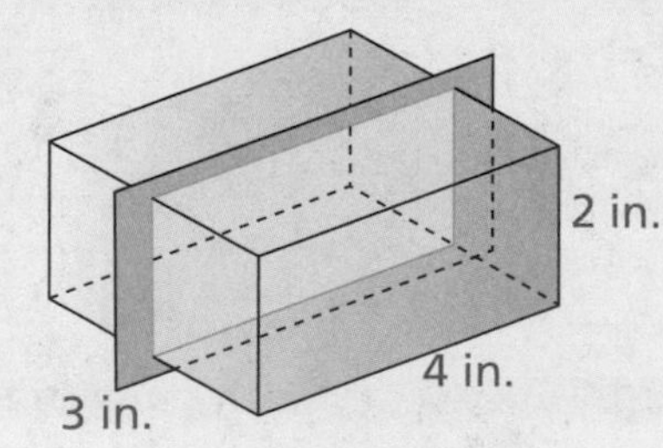

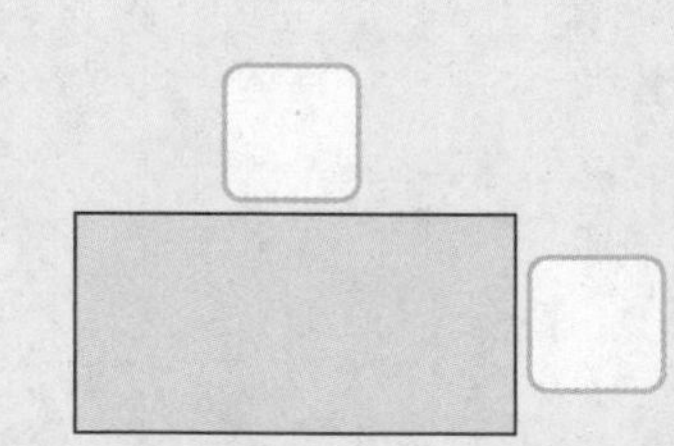

Convince Me! What are the shapes of horizontal and vertical cross sections of a rectangular prism, and how can you determine the dimensions of the cross sections?

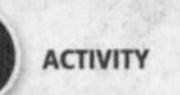

EXAMPLE 2  Describe Cross Sections of Pyramids

Kenya made a sand castle in the shape of a right rectangular pyramid with a height of 0.9 feet.

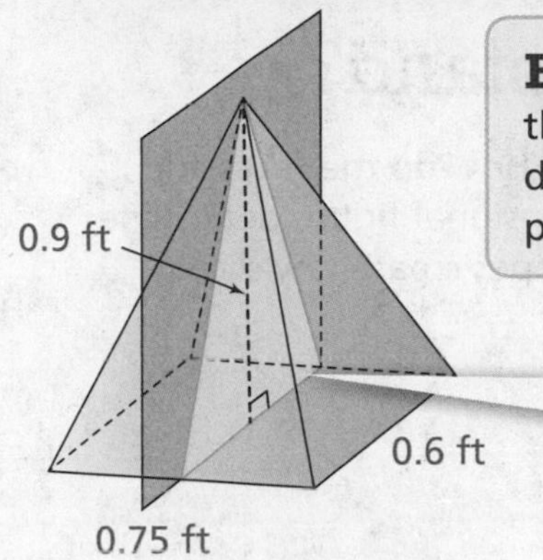

a. If Kenya sliced the castle horizontally, parallel to the base, what would the cross section look like?

Horizontal cross sections are rectangles that are smaller than the base of the pyramid.

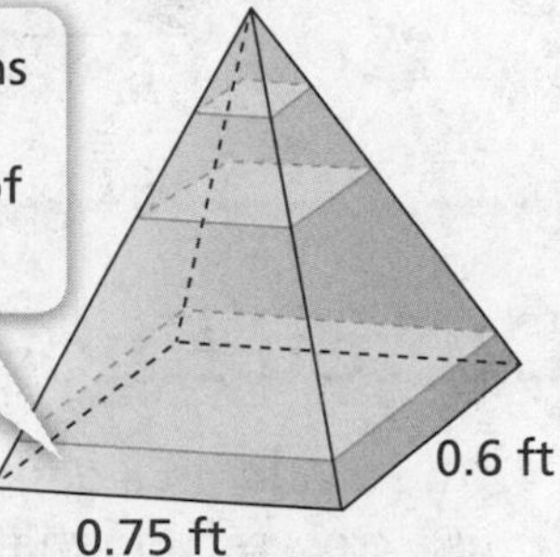

Be Precise How would the horizontal cross section differ if the base of the pyramid were a triangle?

b. If Kenya sliced the castle vertically, through the top vertex, perpendicular to the base, and intersecting the 0.75-foot edges, what would the cross section look like?

0.9 ft

0.6 ft

0.75 ft

The cross section would be an isosceles triangle with a height of 0.9 foot and a base length of 0.6 foot.

EXAMPLE 3  Describe Cross Sections of Cylinders

Jonathan used a mold to make a cylinder out of clay. How can he slice the cylinder to make a rectangular cross section?

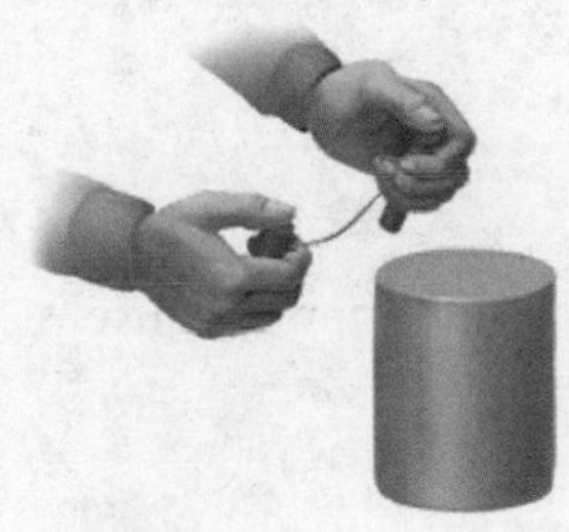

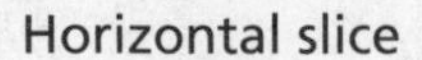

Horizontal slice

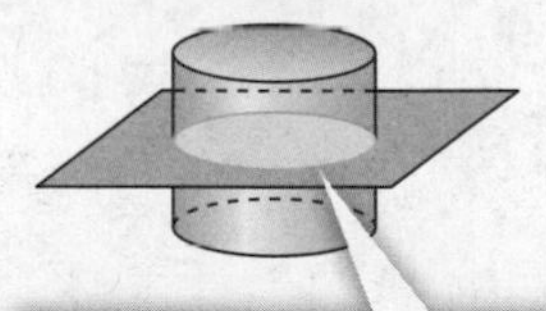

The cross section is parallel to the base, so it is the same size and shape as the base.

Vertical slice

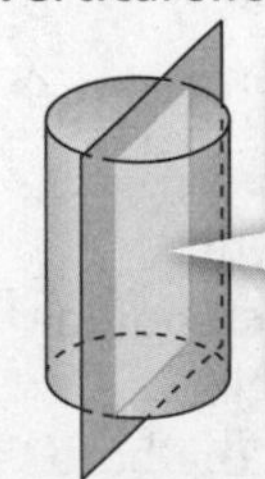

The vertical cross section cut through the center of the circular bases creates a rectangle that is as tall as the cylinder and as wide as the diameter of the circle.

Jonathan should use a vertical slice to create a rectangular cross section.

Try It!

Draw the cross section that is created when a vertical plane intersects the top vertex and the shorter edge of the base of the pyramid shown. What are the dimensions of the cross section?

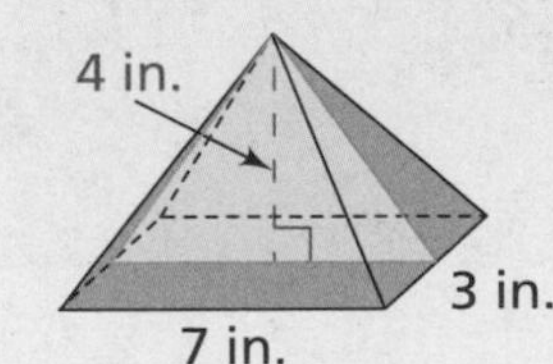

KEY CONCEPT

A cross section is the two-dimensional shape exposed when a three-dimensional figure is sliced.

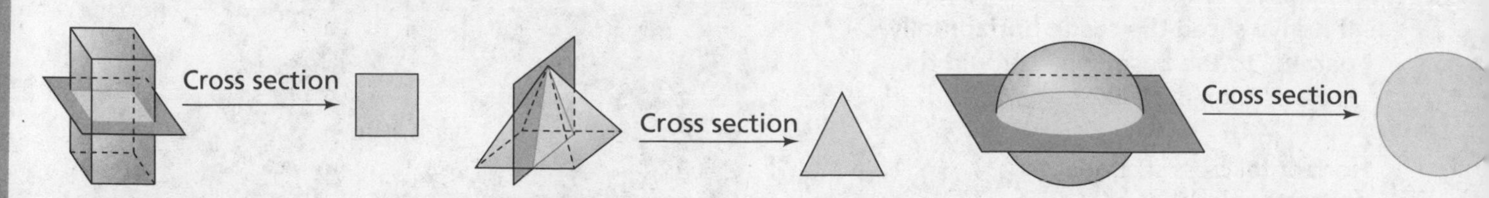

Do You Understand?

1. **Essential Question** How do the faces and surfaces of a three-dimensional figure determine the two-dimensional shapes created by slicing the figure?

2. **Generalize** What is the result when a figure is sliced parallel to the base?

3. **Generalize** What are the shapes of the horizontal cross sections of a right rectangular pyramid? What are the shapes of vertical cross sections through the vertex opposite the base?

Do You Know How?

4. The divider in a desk drawer is a cross section that is parallel to the front of the drawer. What is its shape, and what are its dimensions?

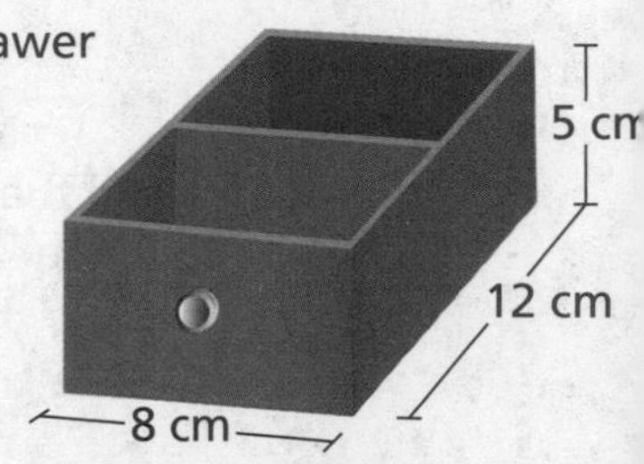

5. Draw the cross section that is formed when the pyramid is sliced vertically through its vertex and its right face, perpendicular to its base.

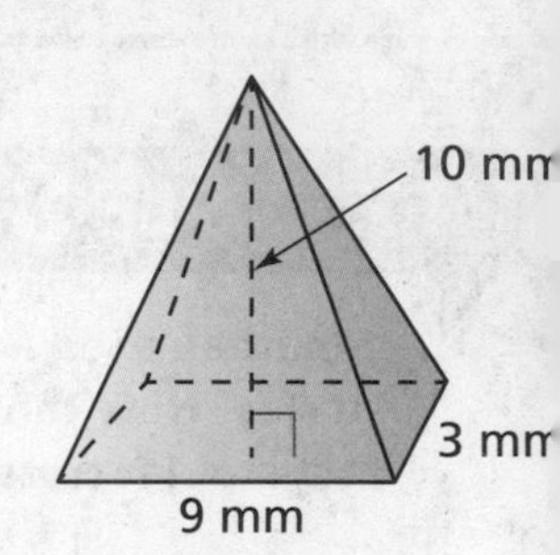

6. What is the shape of the vertical cross section of the cone? What are its dimensions?

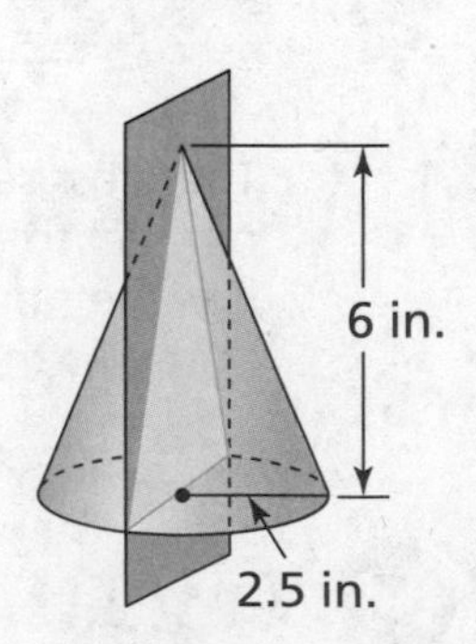

Name: ______________________________

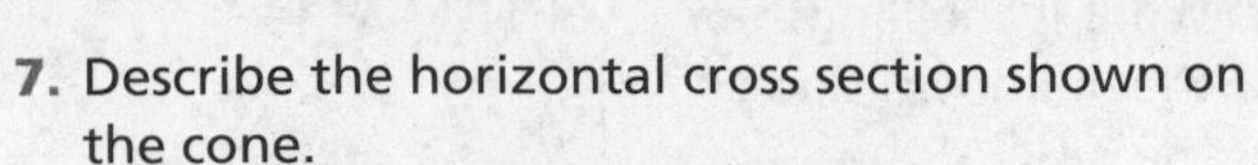

Practice & Problem Solving

Scan for Multimedia

7. Describe the horizontal cross section shown on the cone.

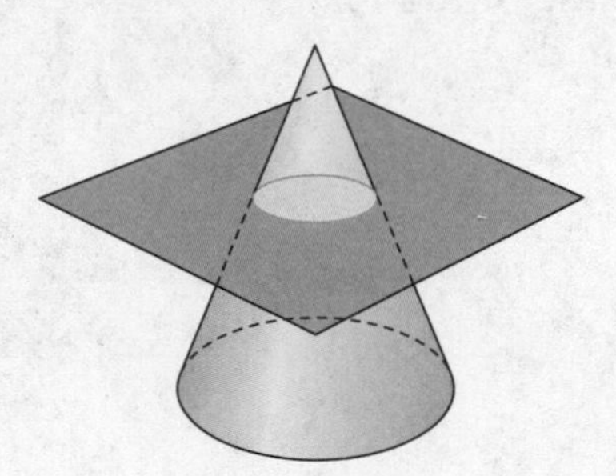

8. Be Precise Describe the cross section that is formed by a vertical plane, perpendicular to the base of the pyramid, that intersects the 9-inch edge and the top vertex of the pyramid shown.

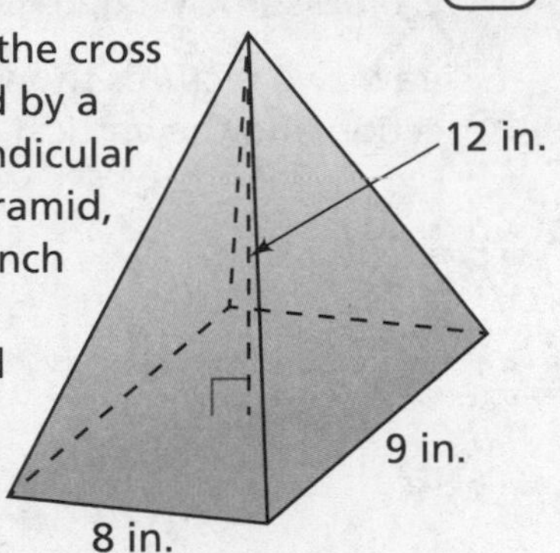

9. Mason is slicing butter for the meal he is preparing. Describe the vertical cross section when the knife slices through the butter, parallel to its sides.

10. a. Look for Relationships What are the dimensions of the vertical cross section?

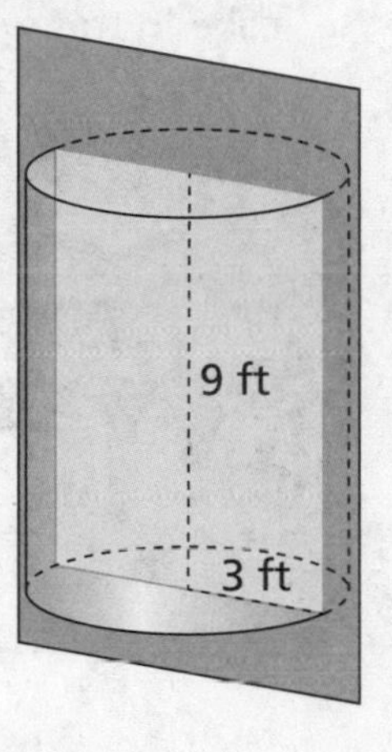

b. Describe the shape of a horizontal cross section.

11. Use the figure shown below.

a. Describe the cross section shown.

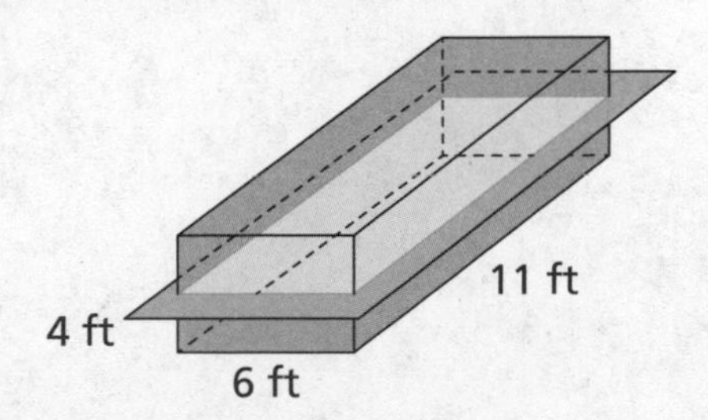

b. Is it possible to have a horizontal cross section with different dimensions if you had the plane intersect the prism at another height? Explain.

12. Make Sense and Persevere The base of a right rectangular pyramid has a length of 12 centimeters and a width of 6 centimeters. Describe the cross section formed by a horizontal plane that intersects the faces of the pyramid above the base.

13. Higher Order Thinking Luis makes blocks from a painted piece of wood with dimensions of 27 inches × 24 inches × 1.5 inches. To make 72 blocks, the wood is cut into 3-inch squares.

Draw two pictures showing the horizontal cross section and the vertical cross section of each block.

14. Make Sense and Persevere The area of the cross section shown is 52 square yards. What is the length of the unknown side of the base of the pyramid?

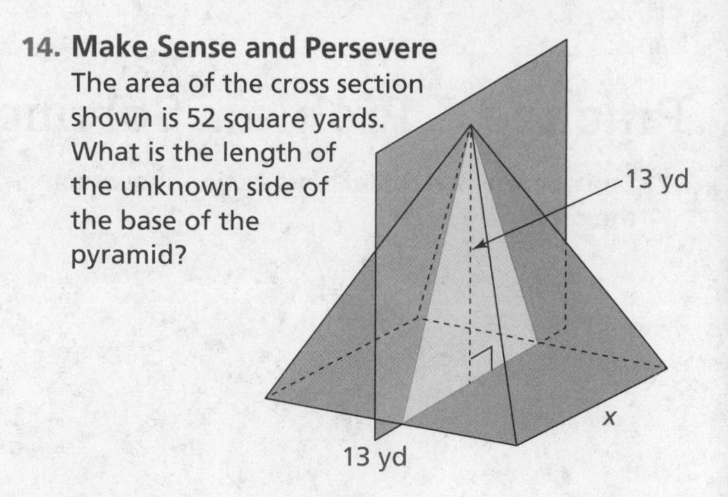

15. A waiter slices a cake shaped like a cylinder with a vertical slice through the center of the cake. Draw the cross section that is made by slicing the cake in this way.

16. Construct Arguments Will all cross sections of a sphere be the same size and shape? Explain.

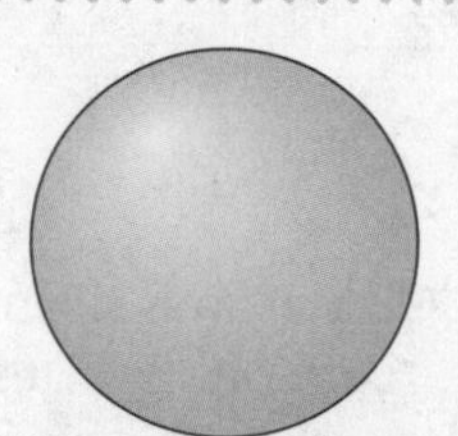

Assessment Practice

17. The horizontal cross section has the same shape and dimensions as which sides of the right rectangular prism? Select all that apply.

- ☐ Top face
- ☐ Left face
- ☐ Back face
- ☐ Bottom face
- ☐ Front face
- ☐ Right face

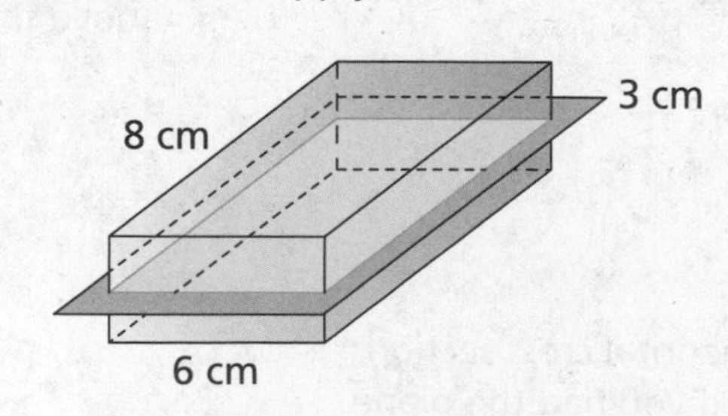

Indiana Lesson 7

Find Volume of Pyramids

Go Online | PearsonRealize.com

I can...
find the volume of pyramids.

Solve & Discuss It!

ACTIVITY

Three identical origami pyramids are used to form a cube-shaped figure like the one shown. How can you describe the volume of each pyramid in terms of the volume of the cube?

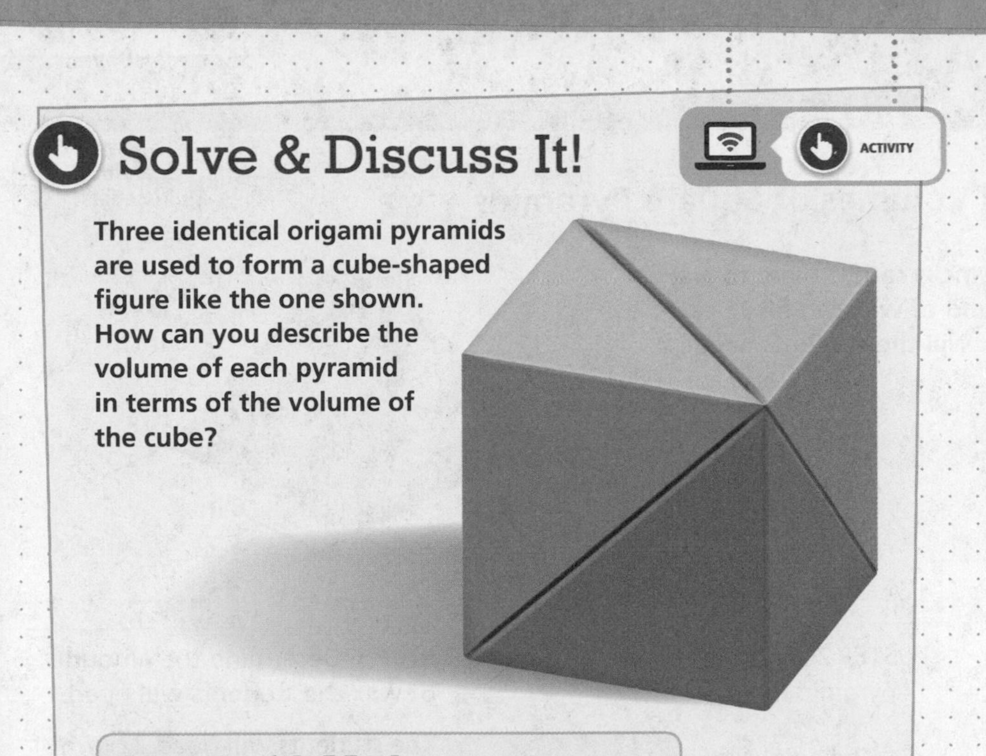

Model with Math How could an equation be used to show the relationship between the volume of each pyramid and the volume of the cube?

Focus on math practices

Look for Relationships How are the length, width, and height dimensions of the cube related to the dimensions of the pyramids?

? Essential Question How is the volume of a prism related to the volume of a pyramid?

EXAMPLE 1  Find Volumes of Square Pyramids

Scan for Multimedia

The students in the art club are using a candle mold to make pyramid-shaped candles. One pound of wax can fill 36 cubic inches. How many pounds of wax will the students need in order to make 50 candles?

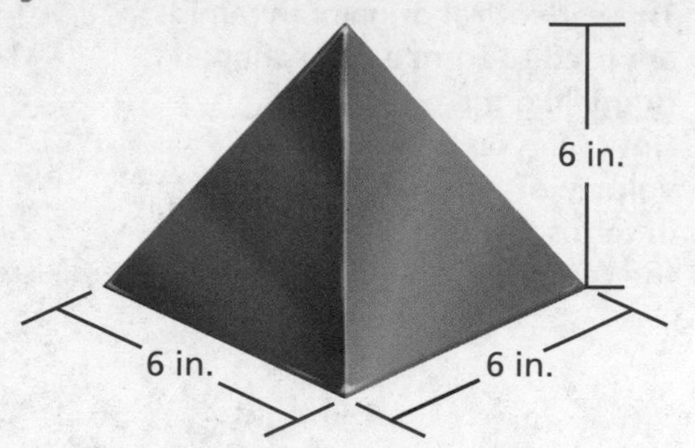

> **Use Structure** How does the volume of the pyramid relate to the volume of a cube?

STEP 1 Determine the formula for the volume of a pyramid.

A cube can be divided into three congruent square pyramids with the same base and height.

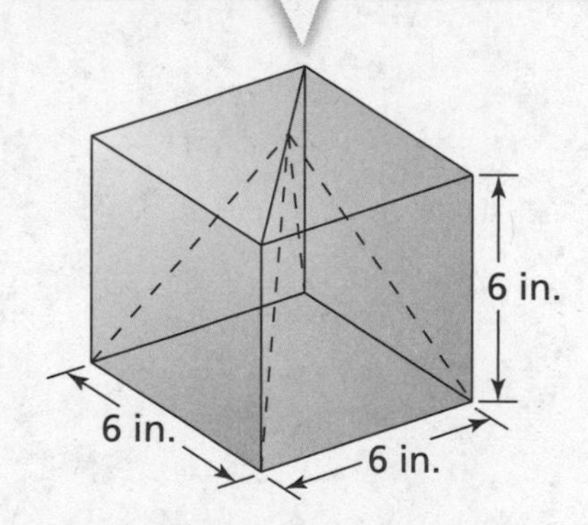

The volume of a rectangular prism is $V = Bh$.

The volume of a pyramid with the same base and height is $V = \frac{1}{3}Bh$.

STEP 2 Find the volume of the pyramid mold.

The height is 6 in.

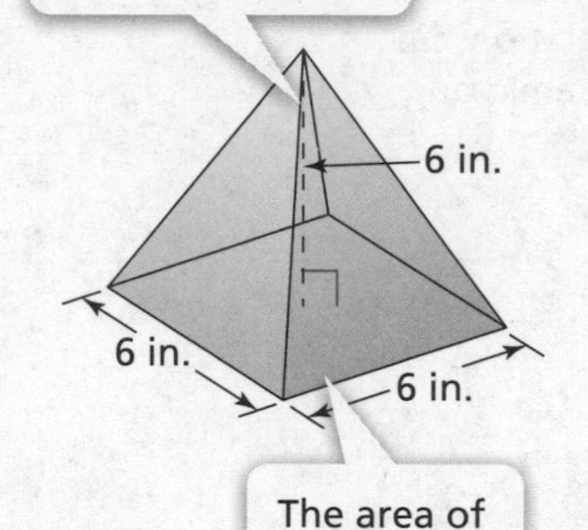

The area of the base is 36 in.^{2}.

$$V = \frac{1}{3}Bh$$
$$= \frac{1}{3}(36 \cdot 6)$$
$$= \frac{216}{3}$$
$$= 72 \text{ in.}^3$$

STEP 3 Determine the amount of wax the students will need.

The students will need 72 in.^{3} of wax for each candle.

$$\frac{36 \text{ in.}^3}{1 \text{ lb of wax}} = \frac{72 \text{ in.}^3}{2 \text{ lb of wax}}$$

The students need 2 pounds of wax for each candle.

The students will need to order 100 pounds of wax to make 50 candles.

Try It!

The art teacher has a second pyramid-shaped candle mold that has a 4-inch square base and a height of 6 inches. How much wax, in cubic inches, is needed to make a candle from the second mold?

The volume of the second mold is

$V = \frac{1}{3}$ ☐ · ☐ = ☐ in.^{3}.

Convince Me! A pyramid-shaped candy mold has the same square base and height as a cube-shaped candy mold. If the cube-shaped candy mold holds 35,937 mm^3 of chocolate, how much chocolate does the pyramid-shaped candy mold hold? Explain.

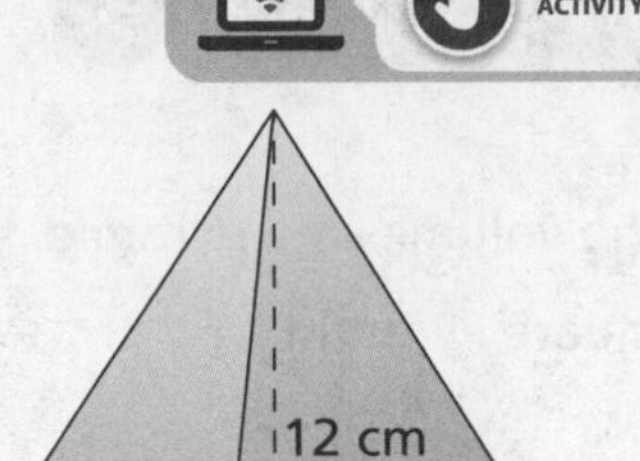

EXAMPLE 2  Find the Volume of Triangular Pyramids

Some students in the art club found a candle mold in the shape of a triangular pyramid. How much wax is needed to fill this mold?

STEP 1 Find the area of the triangular base.

$A = \frac{bh}{2}$

$= \frac{6 \times 8}{2}$

$= 24 \text{ cm}^2$

The area of the base is 24 cm^2.

STEP 2 Find the volume of the pyramid.

$V = \frac{1}{3}Bh$

$= \frac{1}{3} 24 \cdot 12$

$= 96 \text{ cm}^3$

The students will need 96 cm^3 of wax to fill this mold.

How do you find the area of a right triangle?

 Try It!

What is the volume of a triangular pyramid with the dimensions shown?

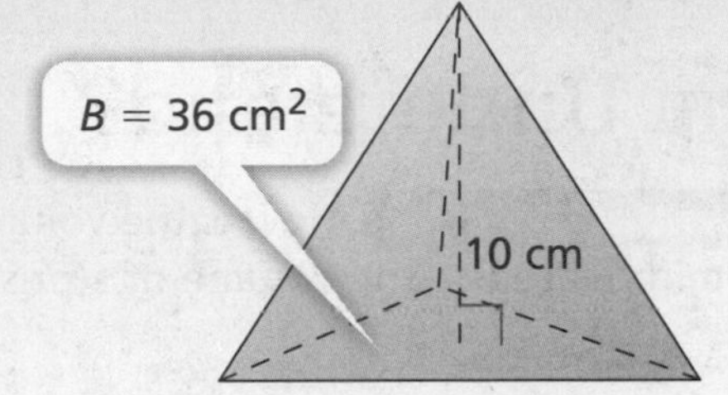

EXAMPLE 3  Solve Problems Involving Volume

What is the volume of the square pyramid shown at the right?

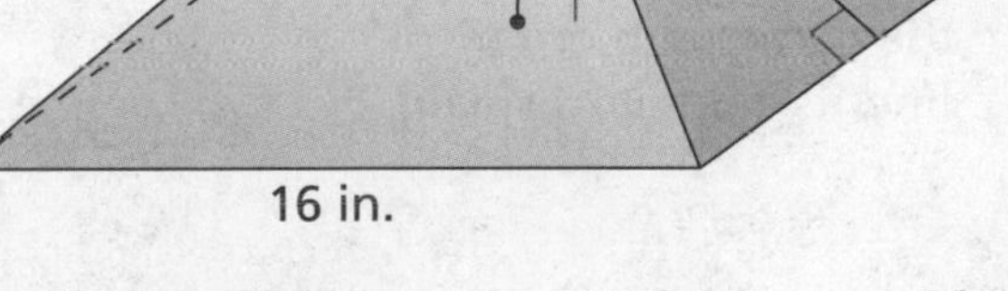

Look for Relationships How can you use what you know about right triangles to find the height of the pyramid?

STEP 1 Use the Pythagorean Theorem to find the height of the pyramid.

This leg of the triangle is the height of the pyramid.

The hypotenuse is the height of the triangular face.

This leg of the triangle is half the length of the base.

h

10 in.

8 in.

$h^2 + 8^2 = 10^2$

$h^2 + 64 = 100$

$h^2 = 36$

$h = \sqrt{36}$

$h = 6$

STEP 2 Find the volume of the pyramid.

$V = \frac{1}{3}Bh$

$V = \frac{1}{3}(16 \cdot 16) \cdot 6$

$V = \frac{1,536}{3}$

$V = 512 \text{ in.}^3$

The volume of the pyramid is 512 in.^3.

 Try It!

What is the volume of the square pyramid shown at the right?

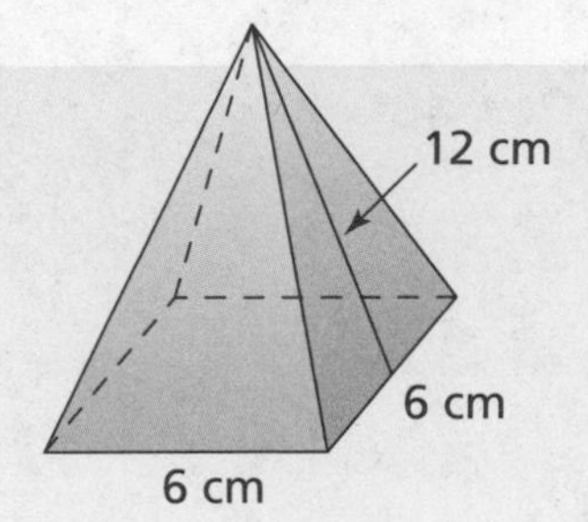

KEY CONCEPT 

To find the volume of a pyramid, you can use the formula $V = \frac{1}{3}Bh$.

Square Pyramid

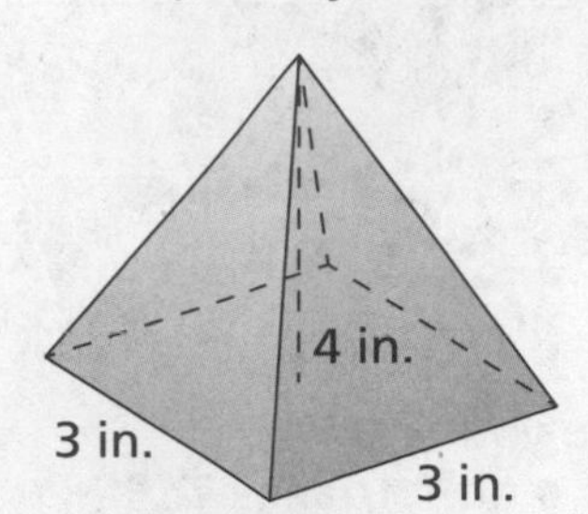

$V = \frac{1}{3}Bh$

$= \frac{1}{3}(9 \cdot 4)$

$= 12 \text{ in.}^3$

Triangular Pyramid

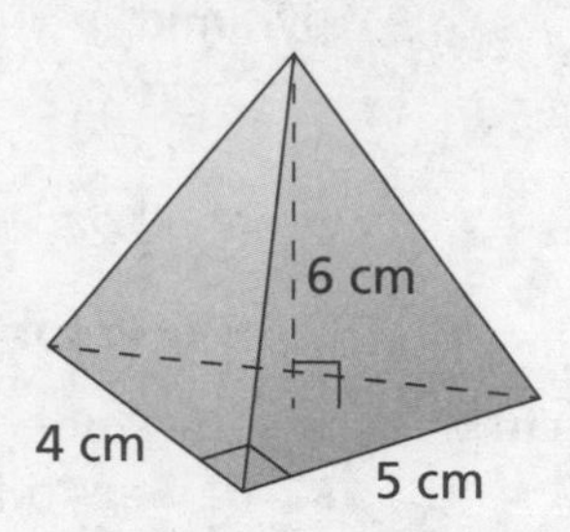

$V = \frac{1}{3}Bh$

$= \frac{1}{3}(10 \cdot 6)$

$= 20 \text{ cm}^3$

Do You Understand?

1. **Essential Question** How is the volume of a pyramid related to the volume of a prism?

2. **Make Sense and Persevere** What additional information do you need to know about the pyramid in order to find its volume? Explain.

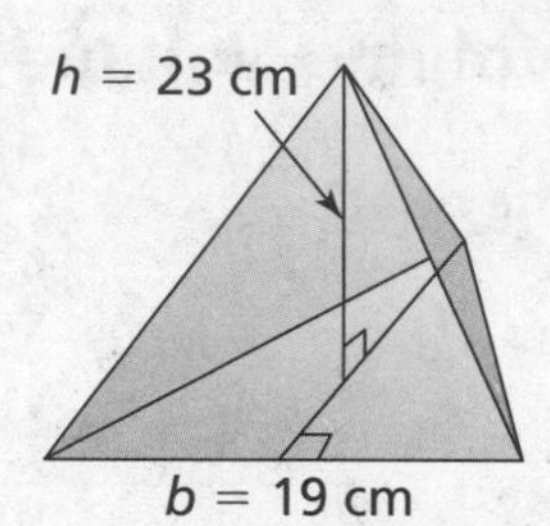

3. How can you use what you know about right triangles to find the height of a triangular face of the pyramid?

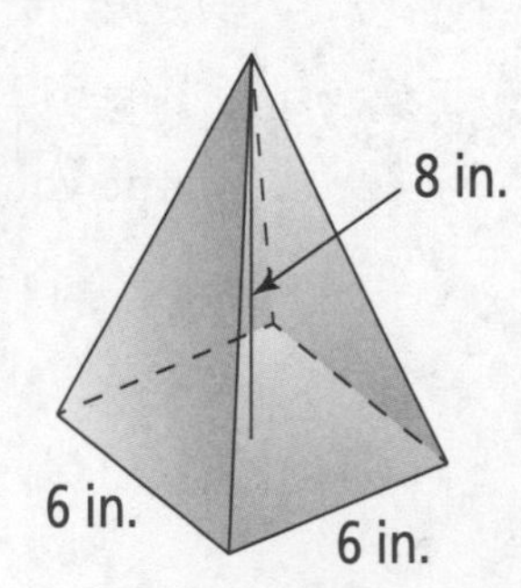

Do You Know How?

4. What is the volume of the square pyramid?

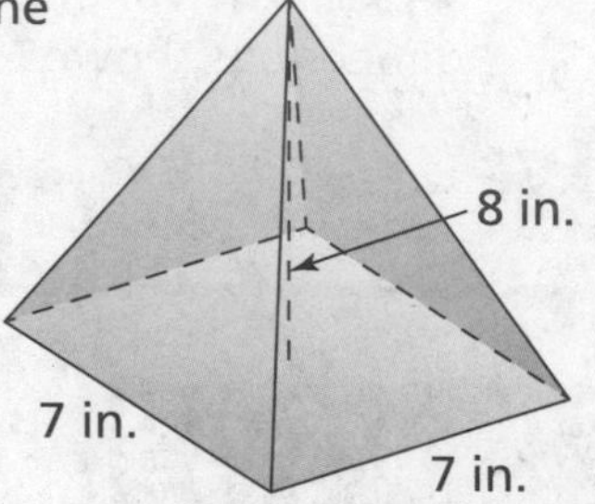

5. What is the volume of the triangular pyramid?

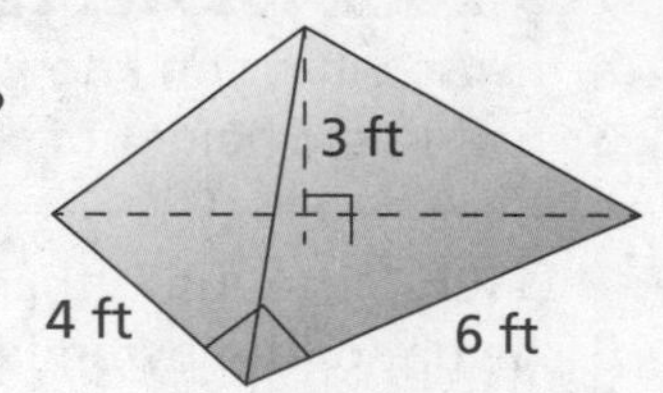

6. Four triangles like the one shown are used to create a pyramid with a square base. What is the volume of the pyramid?

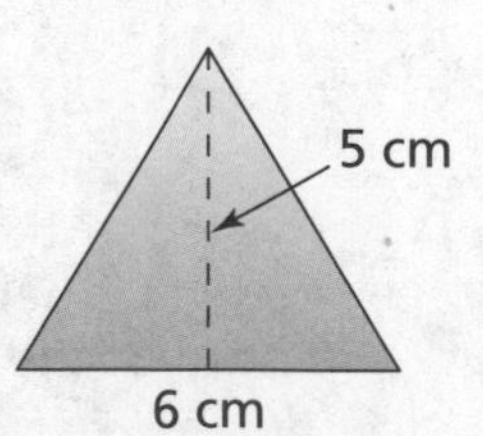

PRACTICE TUTORIAL

Name: ____________________

Practice & Problem Solving  

Scan for Multimedia 

Leveled Practice **In 7–10, find the volume of the pyramids shown.**

7.

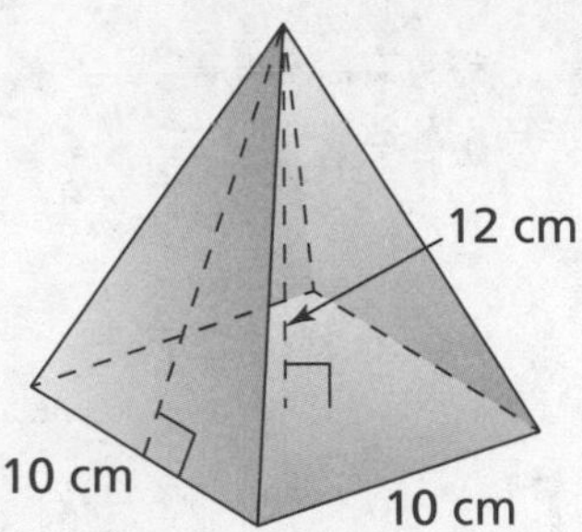

$V = \frac{1}{3}Bh$

$= \frac{1}{3}(\square \cdot \square)$

$= \frac{\square}{3}$

$= \square$ cm^3

8.

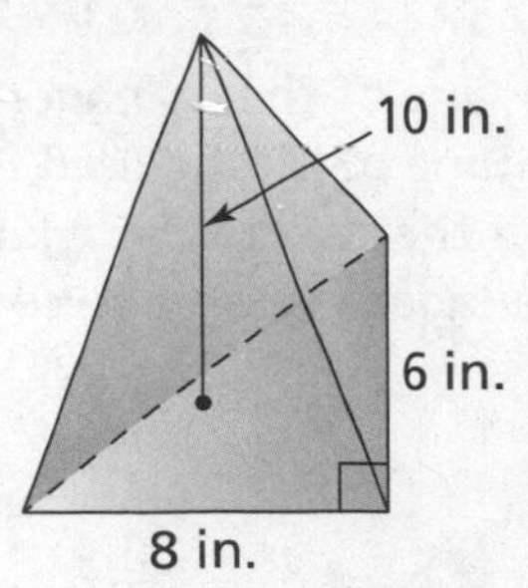

$V = \frac{1}{3}Bh$

$= \frac{1}{3}(\square \cdot \square)$

$= \frac{\square}{3}$ in.^{3}

$= \square$ in.^{3}

9.

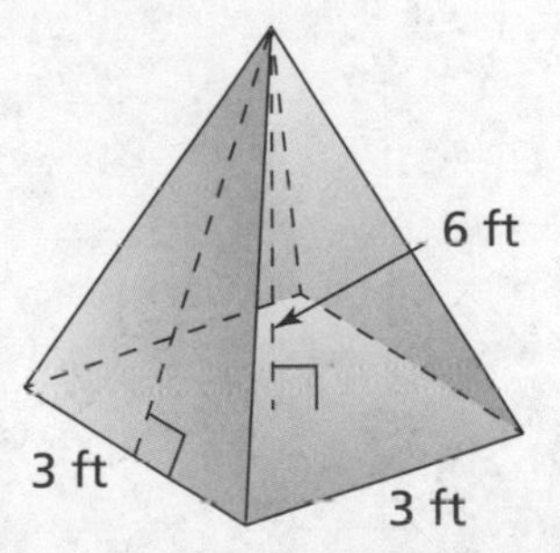

The area of the base of the pyramid is ☐ square feet.
The volume of the pyramid is 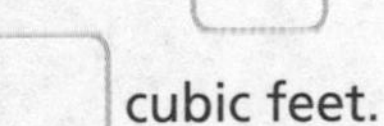 cubic feet.

10.

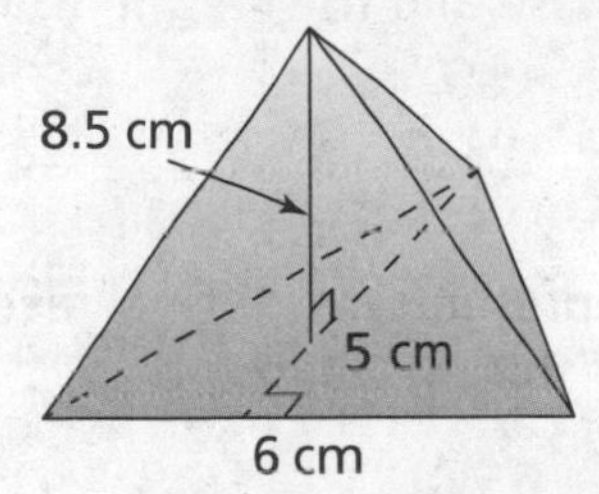

The area of the base of the pyramid is ☐ square centimeters.
The volume of the pyramid is ☐ cubic centimeters.

11. Find the height of the pyramid. Then find the volume.

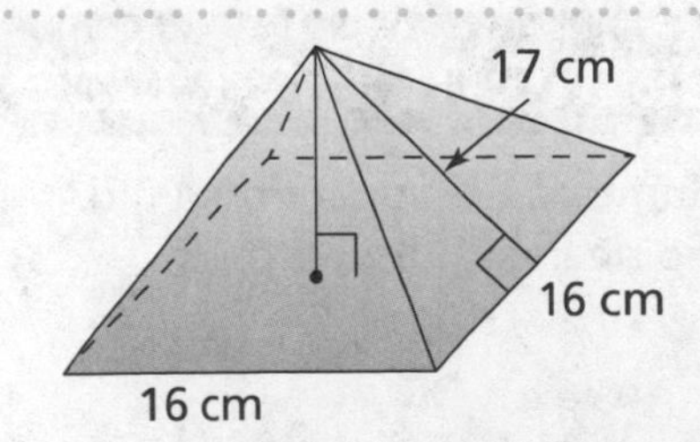

12. **Use Structure** What is the relationship between the volumes of the two pyramids shown? Explain.

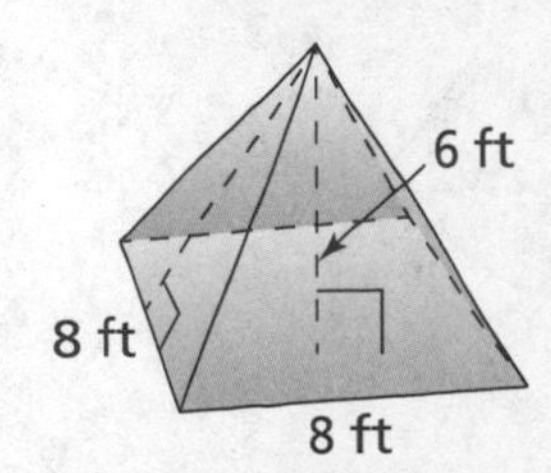

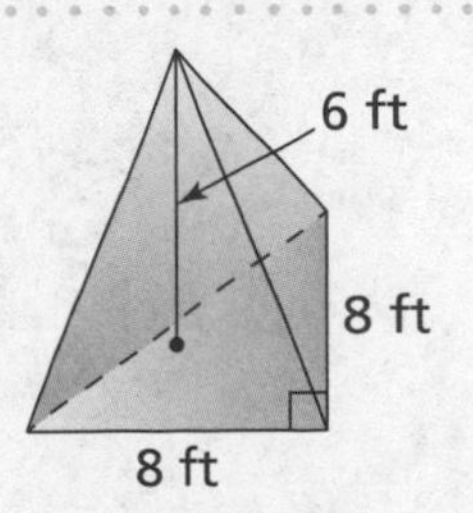

13. A company makes plastic paperweights in the shape of square pyramids.

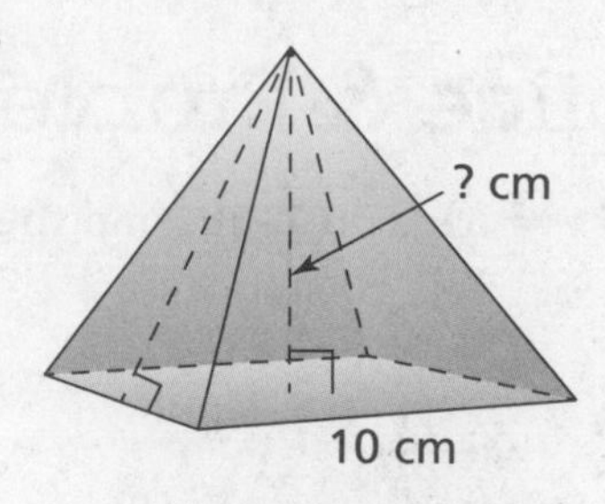

a. Using the base shown, how tall should the pyramid be in order to have a volume of 300 cubic centimeters?

b. **Critique Reasoning** One of the managers suggests that they could cut the volume of plastic used to make the paperweights in half if they cut the side length of the base in half. Is the manager's reasoning correct? Explain.

14. **Higher Order Thinking** Ines made a pyramid out of sand. The volume of her pyramid is 128 in.^{3}. Her pyramid is 6 inches tall.

a. If her pyramid is a square pyramid, what is the side length of the base?

b. If her pyramid is a triangular pyramid, what are possible dimensions of the base and the height of the triangular base?

15. The triangle shown represents one lateral face of a square pyramid. What is the volume of the pyramid?

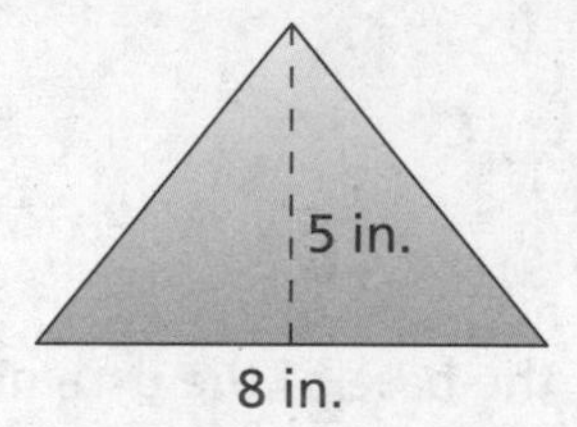

Assessment Practice

16. Find the volume of the square pyramid. Round to the nearest hundredth, if necessary.

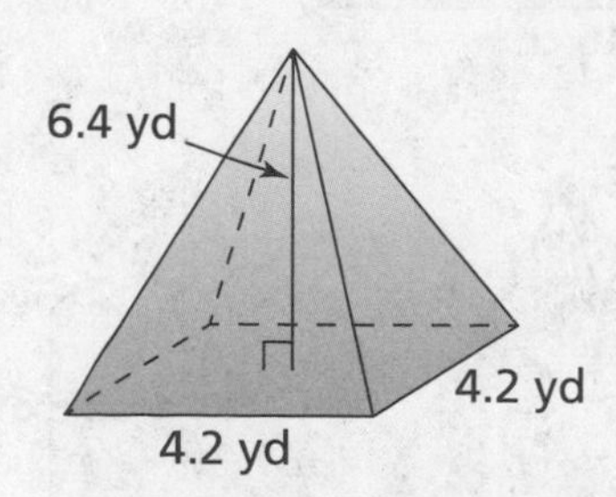

17. Find the volume of the triangular pyramid. Round to the nearest hundredth, if necessary.

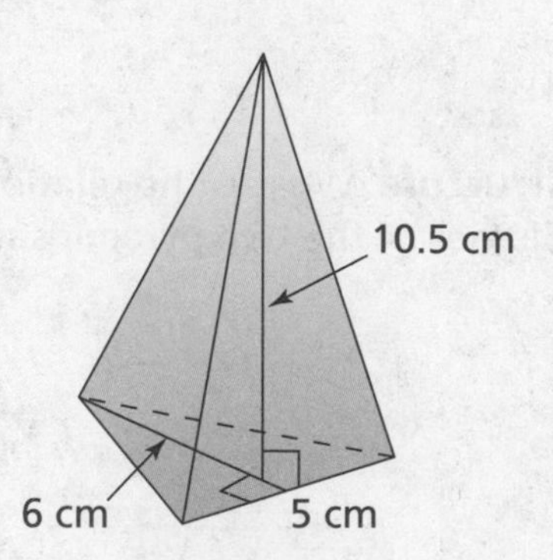